ROADMAP TO SUCCESS
THINK and GROW RICH
WORKBOOK

Author, Janine Loweth

Adapted from NAPOLEON HILL's classic *Think and Grow Rich*

INTRODUCTION

If you have this workbook in hand, you are on your way to making real change in your life, whether that be stepping into a higher level of success, gaining insights into what has prevented you from attaining your intended goals, or perhaps getting clear of your desires and purpose.

This workbook offers a series of action steps that support you in implementing the success principles defined in Napoleon Hill's *Think and Grow Rich* book. It is a roadmap that helps to develop new habits and experience breakthroughs while doing the work exactly as written in spirit and form. The person who can best create results in your life, is you.

Throughout the workbook, you will find content taken directly from the text of *Think and Grow Rich*. Repetition of Napoleon's content is critical to reinforce and solidify your understanding of the concepts. This action will help you focus on the success principles, the roadmap to riches with proven results. As you may know, Napoleon Hill verified those proven results over more than 20 years of interviewing hundreds of wealthy people.

As you progress through the workbook chapter by chapter and in alignment with *Think and Grow Rich*, you'll be reminded of success stories, a defined task, and exercise forms.

Remember shifting habits, expanding your consciousness, and intentionally reprogramming your subconscious mind is a process, a journey of self-discovery and enlightening moments. Be compassionate and patient with yourself as you travel this path. It may be uncomfortable at times, and that is perfectly okay. Resistance is a symptom of growth. It is a sign that you are indeed on the right path, that there is something to learn, and notice. This workbook intends to support and guide you successfully through the process.

Why am I so confident this book will be of value to you? It is because I and countless others have followed the 'Roadmap to Success' that *Think and Grow Rich* offers. The results of which have profoundly impacted our lives. Playing the game of life mindfully and as a team not only expands one's opportunity to gain financial riches, it offers an opportunity to gain a fuller experience of life, connection, support and freedom. It is my wish that you experience the same for yourself. You are worth the investment. You are capable of achieving your dreams. Enjoy the journey.

A message from the Author

My wish for you is that you recognize the greatness within you and the power of your mind. May you experience yourself as someone that is capable of choosing thoughts that serve your life's vision, someone resilient and worthy of success. You have that right. You have that power. Your perception defines your reality, and you are a powerful creator. Leverage the energy within you and choose wisely.

- **Janine M. Loweth**

1

The First Step Towards Riches

DESIRE

The Starting Point of All Achievement

> All achievement, no matter its nature or its purpose, must begin with an intense, burning desire for something definite.

A BURNING DESIRE TO BE AND TO DO

... is the starting point from which the dreamer must take off.
Dreams are not born of indifference, laziness, or lack of ambition.

I bargained with Life for a penny,

And Life would pay no more,

However, I begged in the evening,

When I counted my scanty store.

For Life is a just employer,

He gives you what you ask,

But once you have set the wages,

Why, you must bear the task.

I worked for a menial's hire

Only to learn, dismayed,

That any wage I had asked of Life,

Life would have willingly paid.

TASK 1: DECLARE THE EXACT AMOUNT OF MONEY

First: Fix in your mind the exact amount of money you desire. It is not sufficient merely to say, "I want plenty of money." Be definite as to the amount of money.

$ _____

Why did you choose that exact amount of money? What will you do with the money once it is in your possession? How will it make you feel?

_____
_____
_____
_____
_____
_____
_____
_____
_____
_____
_____
_____
_____
_____
_____
_____
_____
_____
_____
_____
_____

*Only those who become "**Money Conscious**" ever accumulate great riches.*
*"**Money Consciousness**" means that the mind has become so thoroughly saturated with the **DESIRE** for money that one can see one's self already in possession of it.*

Burning Desire

A long while ago, a great warrior faced a situation
which made it necessary for him to make a decision
which ensured his success
on the battlefield.

He was about to send his armies against a powerful
foe whose men outnumbered his own.
He loaded his soldiers into the boats, sailed to the
enemy's country, unloaded soldiers and equipment,
then gave the order to burn the ships
that had carried them.

Addressing his men before the battle, he said:

*"You see the boats going up in smoke.
That means that we cannot leave these shores alive
unless we win. We now have no choice;
we win or we perish!"*

They won.

TASK 2: SET YOUR INTENTION

Second: Determine exactly what you intend to give in return for the money you desire. *There is no such reality as "something for nothing."*

In exchange for the money, I intend to give:

_____
_____
_____
_____
_____
_____
_____
_____
_____
_____
_____

Why did you choose to give in that way? What inspired you? What gifts, talents, skills, interests do you want to offer? For example, I've always wanted to work with children/homeless/the needy; it makes me feel part of a community; it makes me feel generous; it makes me feel like I have something to give.

_____
_____
_____
_____
_____
_____
_____
_____
_____
_____
_____
_____

TASK 3: SPECIFY A BY WHEN DATE

Third: Establish a set date for when you intend to possess the money you desire.

My definite date for acquisition of the money I desire is:

_____

Why have you specified that date? Is there a meaning associated with the date? Is it an important date in your life?

_____
_____
_____
_____
_____
_____
_____
_____
_____
_____
_____
_____
_____
_____
_____
_____

A burning desire has devious ways of transmuting itself into its physical equivalent.

Inspiration

If you think you are beaten, you are,
If you think you dare not, you don't.
If you like to win, but you think you can't,
It is almost certain you won't.

If you think you'll lose, you're lost.
For out of the world we find,
Success begins with a person's will,
It's all in the state of mind.

If you think you are outclassed, you are.
You've got to think high to rise.
You've got to be sure of yourself before
You can ever win a prize.

Life's battles don't always go
To the stronger or faster man,
But sooner or later the person who wins,
Is the one who thinks they can.

TASK 4: A DEFINITE PLAN

Fourth: Create a definite plan for carrying out your desire, and begin at once, whether you are ready or not, to put this plan into action.

My plan of action is:

_____
_____
_____
_____
_____
_____
_____
_____
_____
_____
_____
_____
_____
_____
_____
_____
_____
_____
_____
_____
_____
_____
_____
_____

There is a difference between WISHING for a thing and being READY to receive it. You are never <u>ready</u> for a thing until you <u>believe</u> you can acquire it. The state of mind must be in BELIEF, not mere hope or wish. Open-mindedness is essential for belief. Closed minds do not inspire faith, courage, and belief.

ONE MUST REALIZE THAT ALL WHO HAVE ACCUMULATED GREAT FORTUNES FIRST DID A CERTAIN AMOUNT OF DREAMING, HOPING, WISHING, DESIRING, and PLANNING BEFORE THEY ACQUIRED MONEY.

TASK 5: YOUR STATEMENT OF DESIRE

Fifth: Write out a clear, concise statement of the amount of money you intend to acquire, name the time limit for its acquisition, state what you intend to give in return for the money, and describe clearly the plan through which you intend to accumulate it.

I intend to accumulate_____ in wealth by_____

I intend to accumulate this money in exchange for

_____
_____
_____
_____
_____
_____
_____

My plan of action is to

_____
_____
_____
_____
_____
_____
_____
_____
_____

Signed:_____ Date: _____

TASK 6: READ, MEMORIZE & SAY YOUR STATEMENT OF DESIRE ALOUD TWICE DAILY

Sixth: Read your written statement aloud, twice daily, once just before retiring at night and once after arising in the morning. As you read, SEE, FEEL and BELIEVE yourself ALREADY IN POSSESSION OF THE MONEY.

What does it look like?

_____
_____
_____

What does it feel like to have the money?

_____
_____
_____

Feel the money in your hands. Is the money crisp, or warn and soft?

_____
_____
_____

The steps call for no "hard labor." They call for no "sacrifice." They do not require one to become ridiculous or unthinking. To apply them calls for no great amount of education. The successful completion of these six actions does call for sufficient imagination to enable one to see, and to understand, that accumulation of money cannot be left to chance, good fortune, and luck.

EXERCISE: DREAM, DREAM, DREAM

The Development of Desire

*List your dreams. Without evidence. Without judgement.
Without expectation. Allow yourself to open your mind to possibilities.
Let your imagination fly free.
Know only that whatever you can envision, can in reality, be.*

1. _____
_____
_____
_____

2. _____
_____
_____
_____

3. _____
_____
_____
_____

4. _____
_____
_____
_____

5. _____
_____
_____
_____

EXERCISE: FAILING FORWARD

Transforming Failures into Triumphs

Each of us has felt what it is to be irritated, frustrated or disappointed; the heavy-hearted hand of defeat. The feelings at the moment of failure maybe uncomfortable and yet over time, pass. They are no more in future moments.

Take courage, for these experiences have tempered the spiritual metal of which you are made - they are assets of incomparable value.

It is time to transmute your disappointments into dreams of a constructive nature.

Major Disappointment

1. _____

2. _____

3. _____

Impact on My Growth / The Gifts I've received

1. _____

2. _____

3. _____

SUCCESS REQUIRES NO APOLOGIES, FAILURE PERMITS NO ALIBIS.

Declaration of Faith

Have **Faith** in yourself; **Faith** in the Infinite.

Faith is the "eternal elixir" which gives life, power, and action to the impulse of thought.

Faith is the starting point of all accumulation of riches!

Faith is the basis of all "miracles," and all mysteries which cannot be analyzed by the rules of science!

Faith is the only known antidote for failure.

Faith is the element, the chemical, which when mixed with prayer, gives one direct communication with Infinite Intelligence.

Faith is the element which transforms the ordinary vibration of thought, created by the finite mind of man, into the spiritual equivalent.

Faith is the only agency through which the cosmic forces of Infinite Intelligence can be harnessed and used by man.

2

The Second Step Towards Riches

FAITH

Visualization and Believe in the Attainment of Desire

> Faith is a state of mind which may be induced, or created, by affirmations or repeated instructions to the subconscious mind, through the principles of autosuggestion.

SELF-CONFIDENCE FORMULA'S

> *Autosuggestion is self-suggestion.*

HELPFUL NINJA TIPS...

A. Memorize the order of the opening statements for each self- confidence formula.

I KNOW - I REALIZE - I KNOW - I HAVE - I FULLY REALIZE – I WILL

B. Memorize the formulas in sections. Notice they all use transition words such as "therefore".

C. Repeating them out loud will aid in memorization.

D. Writing and re-writing the statements will aid in memorization.

E. Writing the statements on index cards and reviewing them daily, big yes!

F. Print out 6 copies of the self-confidence formulas and paste them where you will see them every day.

Examples: nightstand, bathroom mirror, shower, at your desk or on a door you use to enter or leave often.

SELF-CONFIDENCE FORMULA
Autosuggestion #1

> **I KNOW** that I have the ability to achieve the object of my definite purpose in life, therefore, I demand of myself persistent, continuous action toward its attainment, and I here and now promise to render such action.

Exercise 1: Take 10 minutes and read this statement aloud over and over again.

Exercise 2: To aid you in your memorization, we have provided the space below to write (and re-write) this statement.

_____
_____
_____
_____
_____
_____
_____
_____
_____
_____
_____
_____
_____
_____
_____
_____
_____
_____

THESE ARE ONLY WORDS UNTIL YOU CLAIM THEM WITH YOUR EMOTION AND MAKE THEM YOUR OWN. EACH TIME YOU REPEAT IT, TRY TO MEMORIZE ONE ADDITIONAL PHRASE UNTIL AT THE END OF YOUR RECITATION, YOU HAVE MEMORIZED THE SENTENCE.

Success Story

MAHATMA GANDHI

Gandhi wields more potential power than any man living at his time. How did he come by that power?

Gandhi has accomplished, through the influence of faith, that which the strongest military power on earth could not, and never will accomplish through soldiers and military equipment. He had accomplished the astounding feat of influencing 200 million minds to coalesce and move in unison as a single mind.

What other force on earth, except faith, could do as much?

SELF-CONFIDENCE FORMULA
Autosuggestion #2

> **I REALIZE** the dominating thoughts of my mind will eventually reproduce themselves in outward, physical action and gradually transform themselves into physical reality, therefore, I will concentrate my thoughts for thirty minutes daily, upon the task of thinking of the person I intend to become, thereby creating in my mind a clear mental picture of that person.

Exercise 1: Take 10 minutes and read this statement aloud over and over again.

Exercise 2: To aid you in your memorization, we have provided the space below to write (and re-write) this statement.

_____
_____
_____
_____
_____
_____
_____
_____
_____
_____
_____
_____
_____
_____
_____
_____

*THESE ARE ONLY WORDS UNTIL YOU CLAIM THEM WITH YOUR EMOTION AND MAKE THEM YOUR OWN.
EACH TIME YOU REPEAT IT, TRY TO MEMORIZE ONE ADDITIONAL PHRASE UNTIL,
AT THE END OF YOUR RECITATION, YOU HAVE MEMORIZED THE SENTENCE.*

Any idea, plan, or purpose
may be placed in the mind
through repetition of thought.

Thoughts which are mixed with
any of the feelings of emotions
constitute a magnetic force
which attracts
other similar or related thoughts.

SELF-CONFIDENCE FORMULA
Autosuggestion #3

> **I KNOW** through the principal of autosuggestion, any desire that I persistently hold in my mind will eventually seek expression through some practical means of attaining the object back of it, therefore, I will devote ten minutes daily to demanding of myself the development of self-confidence.

Exercise 1: Take 10 minutes and read this statement aloud over and over again.

Exercise 2: To aid you in your memorization, we have provided the space below to write (and re-write) this statement.

THESE ARE ONLY WORDS UNTIL YOU CLAIM THEM WITH YOUR EMOTION AND MAKE THEM YOURS. EACH TIME YOU REPEAT IT, TRY TO MEMORIZE ONE ADDITIONAL PHRASE UNTIL, AT THE END OF YOUR RECITATION, YOU HAVE MEMORIZED THE SENTENCE.

SELF-CONFIDENCE FORMULA
Autosuggestion #4

> **I HAVE** clearly written down a description of my definite chief aim in life, and I will never stop trying until I have developed sufficient self-confidence for its attainment.

Exercise 1: Take 10 minutes and read this statement aloud over and over again.

Exercise 2: To aid you in your memorization, we have provided the space below to write (and re-write) this statement.

_____
_____
_____
_____
_____
_____
_____
_____
_____
_____
_____
_____
_____
_____
_____
_____
_____
_____
_____
_____
_____
_____

THESE ARE ONLY WORDS UNTIL YOU CLAIM THEM WITH YOUR EMOTION AND MAKE THEM YOUR OWN.
EACH TIME YOU REPEAT IT, TRY TO MEMORIZE ONE ADDITIONAL PHRASE UNTIL
AT THE END OF YOUR RECITATION, YOU HAVE MEMORIZED THE SENTENCE.

SELF-CONFIDENCE FORMULA
Autosuggestion #5

> **I FULLY REALIZE** that no wealth or position can long endure unless built on truth and justice; therefore, I will engage in no transaction that does not benefit all whom it affects.
>
> I will succeed by attracting to myself the forces I wish to use and the cooperation of other people. I will induce others to serve me because of my willingness to serve others.
>
> I will eliminate hatred, envy, jealousy, selfishness and cynicism by developing love for all humanity - because I know that a negative attitude toward others can never bring me success.
>
> I will cause others to believe in me because I will believe in them, and myself.

Exercise 1: Take 10 minutes and read this statement aloud over and over again.

Exercise 2: To aid you in your memorization, we have provided the space below to write (and re-write) this statement.

_____
_____
_____
_____
_____
_____
_____
_____
_____
_____
_____
_____

THESE ARE ONLY WORDS UNTIL YOU CLAIM THEM WITH YOUR EMOTION AND MAKE THEM YOUR OWN. EACH TIME YOU REPEAT IT, TRY TO MEMORIZE ONE ADDITIONAL PHRASE UNTIL AT THE END OF YOUR RECITATION, YOU HAVE MEMORIZED THE SENTENCE.

Like the wind which carries one ship
east and another west, the law of
autosuggestion will lift you up or
pull you down, according to
the way you set your
sails of thought.

SELF-CONFIDENCE FORMULA
Autosuggestion #6

> **I WILL** sign my name to this formula, commit it to memory, and repeat it aloud once a day, with full FAITH that it will gradually influence my THOUGHTS and ACTIONS so that I will become a self-reliant and successful person.

Exercise 1: Take 10 minutes and read this statement aloud over and over again.

Exercise 2: To aid you in your memorization, we have provided the space below to write (and re-write) this statement.

_____
_____
_____
_____
_____
_____
_____
_____
_____
_____
_____
_____
_____

Signed:_____ Date:_____

SELF-CONFIDENCE FORMULAS

1. **I KNOW** that I have the ability to achieve the object of my definite purpose in life, therefore, I demand of myself persistent, continuous action toward its attainment, and I here and now, promise to render such action.

2. **I REALIZE** the dominating thoughts of my mind will eventually reproduce themselves in outward, physical action and gradually transform themselves into physical reality, therefore, I will concentrate my thoughts for thirty minutes daily, upon the task of thinking of the person I intend to become, thereby creating in my mind, a clear mental picture of that person.

3. **I KNOW** through the principal of autosuggestion, any desire that I persistently hold in my mind will eventually seek expression through some practical means of attaining the object back of it, therefore, I will devote ten minutes daily to demanding of myself the development of self-confidence.

4. **I HAVE** clearly written down a description of my definite chief aim in life, and I will never stop trying until I have developed sufficient self-confidence for its attainment.

5. **I FULLY REALIZE** that no wealth or position can long endure unless built on truth and justice; therefore, I will engage in no transaction that does not benefit all whom it affects. I will succeed by attracting to myself the forces I wish to use and the cooperation of other people. I will induce others to serve me because of my willingness to serve others. I will eliminate hatred, envy, jealousy, selfishness and cynicism by developing love for all humanity - because I know that a negative attitude toward others can never bring me success. I will cause others to believe in me because I will believe in them, and myself.

6. **I WILL** sign my name to this formula, commit it to memory, and repeat it aloud once a day, with full FAITH that it will gradually influence my THOUGHTS and ACTIONS so that I will become a self-reliant and successful person.

"The grateful mind continually expects good things, and expectations become faith."

"Desire backed by faith knows no such word as impossible."

"Faith and Fear make poor bedfellows. Where one is found, the other cannot exist."

"The greatest application of applied faith is learning the art of keeping your mind focused on what you want."

3

The Third Step Towards Riches

AUTOSUGGESTION

The Medium for Influencing the Subconscious Mind

> Autosuggestion is self-suggestion. Communicate the object of your desire directly to your subconscious mind in a spirit of absolute faith. Through repetition of this procedure, you voluntarily create thought habits which are favorable to your efforts to transmute desire into its monetary equivalent.
>
> You are now reading the chapter which represents the keystone to the arch of this philosophy. The instructions contained in this chapter must be understood and applied with persistence, if you succeed in transmuting desire into money.

TASK 1: UNDERSTANDING THE SUBCONSCIOUS

> The Subconscious Mind consists of a field of consciousness, in which every impulse of thought that reaches the objective mind through any of the five senses, is classified and recorded. Essentially stating that our subconscious mind, although unrecognized by our conscious mind, is aware of all thoughts and feelings and experiences.
>
> Whether we as human beings consciously notice information or not, our subconscious mind continuously records our thoughts, all thoughts triggered by what we hear, see, touch, smell or taste whether involuntary or voluntarily seeded.
>
> It receives, and files, sense impressions or thoughts, regardless of their nature therefore, you may voluntarily plant in your subconscious mind and DESIRE, plan, thought or purpose which you want to translate into its physical or monetary equivalent.

List 3 to 5 of the dominating thoughts you experience often. For-example, 'Life is hard', 'I'm unlucky', 'I'm too young/old', thoughts about relationships, thoughts relating money, etc.

_____
_____
_____
_____
_____
_____
_____
_____
_____
_____
_____
_____
_____

IF YOU FAIL TO PLANT DESIRES IN YOUR SUBCONSCIOUS MIND, IT WILL FEED UPON THE THOUGHTS THAT REACH IT AS A RESULT OF YOUR NEGLECT.

TASK 2: GUARDING YOUR THOUGHTS

> Through the 'dominating thoughts' which we permit to occupy our mind (whether they be negative or positive thoughts), the principal of autosuggestion voluntarily or involuntarily reaches the subconscious mind and influences it with those thoughts.
>
> All sense impressions which are perceived through the five senses are captured and processed by the conscious thinking mind and may be either passed on to the subconscious mind or rejected at will. The conscious faculty serves as an outer guard at the approach to the subconscious.

What are the thoughts and beliefs you've heard others (family, friends, colleagues, the news, the community, acquaintances) say or repeat, which you need to guard your mind against?

_____
_____
_____
_____
_____
_____
_____
_____
_____
_____
_____
_____
_____
_____
_____
_____
_____
_____
_____
_____

PEOPLE MAY BECOME THE MASTER OF THEMSELVES AND OF THEIR ENVIRONMENT, BECAUSE THEY HAVE THE POWER TO INFLUENCE THEIR OWN SUBCONSCIOUS MIND, AND THROUGH IT, GAIN THE COOPERATION OF INFINITE INTELLIGENCE.

TASK 3: GUARDING YOUR THOUGHTS

Weeding Your Mental Garden

What are the dominant thoughts you feel have most influenced your life in a negative way; thoughts that have held you small, weighed heavily on you, affected how you feel and/or see yourself or others, or limited your success?

_____
_____
_____
_____
_____
_____
_____
_____
_____
_____
_____
_____
_____

Feeding your Mental Garden

What are the replacement thoughts you will consciously choose for yourself moving forward? What thoughts will you seed in place of the weeds above?

_____
_____
_____
_____
_____
_____
_____
_____
_____
_____
_____
_____
_____

Skepticism, in connection with ALL new ideas, is a characteristic of all human beings. If, however, you follow the instructions outlined by Napoleon Hill, your skepticism will be replaced by belief, and this, in turn, will soon become crystallized into absolute faith.

Then you will have arrived at the point where you may truly say,

"I am the master of my fate, I am the captain of my soul!"

TASK 4: THE PRACTICE OF EMOTIONALIZING YOUR BELIEF

Below are a series of positive affirmations.
Select the ones that excite you most and/or create some of your own.

Quick Tip: *Say the affirmation/s 100 times each day while moving your body. Introducing music can help to emotionalize the seeded thoughts. Affirmations need to be positive, present and in the first person.*

I am open to receive all of life's gifts now.

Money flows to me easily and abundantly.

I am healthy, peaceful, joyful and energized.

I accept myself and know that I am worthy of success.

Day by day, in every way, I am getting better and better.

I am in constant communication with my creative source.

I have the energy I need to accomplish my goals and to fulfill my desires.

BELIEF IS A RESULT OF REPETITION. BREATHE, FEEL AND REPEAT THE WORDS UNTIL WHAT IS UNCOMFORTABLE TRANSFORMS ITSELF INTO POWERFUL BELIEF.

EMOTIONALIZING YOUR BELIEFS

When reading aloud the statement of your desire through which you are endeavoring to develop a "money consciousness", the mere reading of the words is of no consequence unless you mix emotion or feeling with your words. If you repeat the famous Émile Coué formula, "Day by day, in every way, I am getting better and better", a million times without mixing emotion and faith with your words, you will experience no desirable results. Your subconscious mind only recognizes and acts upon thoughts that have been blended with emotions or feeling.

This is a fact of such importance as to warrant repetition in practically every chapter because the lack of understanding of this point is the main reason why the majority of people who try to apply the principles of autosuggestion receive no desirable results.

Plain, unemotional words do not influence the subconscious mind. You will get no appreciable results until you learn to reach your subconscious mind with thoughts, or words which have been well emotionalized with belief.

TASK 5: YOUR STATEMENT OF PURPOSE

<u>Fill in the blanks to create your STATEMENT OF PURPOSE</u>

By the (#)____day of (month)_____, (year)_____, I will have in my possession (sum) $_____, which will come to me in various amounts from time to time during the interim. In return for this money I will give the most efficient service of which I am capable, rendering the fullest possible quantity, and the best possible quantity of service in the capacity of (describe service or merchandise)

_____
_____
_____
_____
_____
_____
_____
_____

I believe that I will have this money in my possession. My faith is so strong that I can now see this money before my eyes. I can touch it with my hands. It is now awaiting transfer to me at the time and in the proportion that I deliver the service I intend to render in return for it. I am awaiting a plan by which to accumulate this money and I will follow that plan when it is received.

First: Go into some quiet spot (preferably in bed at night) where you will not be disturbed or interrupted, close your eyes, and repeat aloud (so you may hear your own words) the written statement of the amount of money you intend to accumulate, the time limit for its accumulation, and a description of the service or merchandise you intend to give in return for the money. As you carry out these instructions - SEE YOURSELF ALREADY IN POSSESSION OF THE MONEY.

Second: Repeat this program morning and night until you can clearly visualize (in your imagination) the money you intend to accumulate.

Third: Place a written copy of your Statement of Purpose where you can see it night and morning and read it just before retiring and upon arising until it has been memorized. **Example:** nightstand by your bed or mirror in your bathroom.

DISTINCTIONS AROUND TERMINOLOGY

YOUR DESIRE

Your Passion – Your Dream – Your Joy

DEFINITE CHIEF AIM

YOUR DESIRE + VISION

1. Your $$$ Intention
2. By When
3. What You Are Willing to Give in Exchange
4. What You Are Creating
5. What You Intend to Use The $$$ For

STATEMENT OF DESIRE

YOUR DESIRE + VISION + FAITH

"By the first day of _____, _____20_____, I will have in my possession $_____, which will come to me in various amounts from time to time during the interim.

"In return for this money I will give the most efficient service of which I am capable, rendering the fullest possible quantity, and the best possible quality of service in the capacity of selling _____.
(Describe the service or merchandise you intend to sell.)

"I believe that I will have this money in my possession. My faith is so strong that I can now see this money before my eyes. I can touch it with my hands. It is now awaiting transfer to me at the time, and in the proportion that I deliver the service I intend to render in return for it. I am awaiting a plan by which to accumulate this money, and I will follow that plan, when it is received."

STATEMENT OF PURPOSE

4

The Fourth Step Towards Riches

SPECIALIZED KNOWLEDGE

Personal Experiences or Observations

> Knowledge will not attract money unless it is organized and intelligently directed, through practical plans of action, to the definite end of accumulation of money. Knowledge is only potential power. It becomes power only when, and if, it is organized into definite plans of action, and directed to a definite end. Any man is educated who knows where to get knowledge when he needs it, and how organized that knowledge into definite plans of action.

Specialized Knowledge

Thomas A. Edison had only three months of "schooling." Henry Ford had less than a sixth-grade "schooling". Before you can be sure of your ability to transmute desire into its monetary equivalent, you will require specialized knowledge of the service, merchandise, or profession which you intend to offer in return for fortune. Perhaps you may need much more specialized knowledge than you have the ability or the inclination to acquire, and if this should be, you may bridge your weakness through the aid of your "Mastermind" group.

The accumulation of great fortunes calls for power, and power is acquired through highly organized and intelligently directed specialized knowledge, but that knowledge does not necessarily have to be in the possession of the man who accumulates the fortune.

The preceding paragraph should give hope and encouragement to the person with ambition to accumulate a fortune, who has not possessed themselves the necessary "education" to supply such specialized knowledge as he/she may require.

TASK 1: WHAT YOU NEED TO KNOW

> ***First***: Decide the sort of specialized knowledge you require, the purpose for which it is needed, and where you can attain it.

1. What is the goal you are working to achieve?
   _____
   _____
   _____
   _____
   _____

2. What information is required to achieve the object of your desires?
   _____
   _____
   _____
   _____
   _____

3. What aspects (skills and knowledge) from your own experiences and/or education will support your endeavor?
   _____
   _____
   _____
   _____
   _____

4. What information (facts, processes, resources, etc.) do you need to find in order to achieve your definite chief aim?
   _____
   _____
   _____
   _____
   _____

THE BEGINNING OF ANY SUCCESSFUL BUSINESS IS AN IDEA! BACK OF ALL IDEAS, IS SPECIALIZED KNOWLEDGE.

TASK 2: WHERE TO FIND SPECIALIZED KNOWLEDGE

> *Second*: Determine where you can attain the knowledge required to achieve your goals.

1. What experience or education is available to you through the cooperation of others (a Mastermind Alliance)?
   _____
   _____
   _____
   _____
   _____
   _____

2. What specialized knowledge is attainable through colleges or universities?
   _____
   _____
   _____
   _____
   _____
   _____

3. What specialized knowledge is available in libraries (I.e. books/journals)?
   _____
   _____
   _____
   _____
   _____
   _____

4. What courses could you take to attain specialized knowledge (online, night school, seminars etc.)?
   _____
   _____
   _____
   _____
   _____
   _____

KNOWLEDGE IS ONLY POTENTIAL POWER. IT BECOMES POWER ONLY WHEN IT IS ORGANIZED INTO DEFINITE PLANS OF ACTION AND DIRECTED TO A DEFINITE END.

TASK 3: WHO TO CONTACT

List the name and contact information to those people or organizations who can provide you the specialized knowledge you require to meet your goals.

Organization:_____ Date Contacted: _____
Contact Name: _____ Investment Fee: _____
Phone Number: _____ Next Steps: _____

Email:_____
Website:_____
Address: _____
_____

Organization:_____ Date Contacted: _____
Contact Name: _____ Investment Fee: _____
Phone Number: _____ Next Steps: _____

Email:_____
Website:_____
Address: _____
_____

Organization:_____ Date Contacted: _____
Contact Name: _____ Investment Fee: _____
Phone Number: _____ Next Steps: _____

Email:_____
Website:_____
Address: _____
_____

Organization:_____ Date Contacted: _____
Contact Name: _____ Investment Fee: _____
Phone Number: _____ Next Steps: _____

Email:_____
Website:_____
Address: _____
_____

5

The Fifth Step Towards Riches

IMAGINATION

The Workshop of The Mind

> The imagination is literally the workshop wherein are fashioned all plans created by man. The impulse, the desire, is given shape, form, and action through the aid of the imaginative faculty of the mind. It has been said that man can create anything which he can imagine.
>
> Of all the ages of civilization, this is the most favorable for the development of the imagination because it is an age of rapid change. On every hand one may contact stimuli which develop the imagination.

TASK 1: CULTIVATE IMAGINATION

> Our own brains are both a broadcasting and a receiving station for the 'vibration of thought'. Our only limitation, lies within the development and use of our imagination.
>
> Desire is only a thought, an impulse. It is nebulous and ephemeral. It is an abstract, and of no value, until it has been transformed into its physical counterpart.

List your desires below from the perspective of 'anything' is possible.

WHO I WANT TO BE:
_____
_____
_____
_____
_____

WHAT I WANT TO EXPERIENCE:
_____
_____
_____
_____
_____

WHAT I WANT TO HAVE:
_____
_____
_____
_____
_____

WHERE I WANT TO GO:
_____
_____
_____
_____
_____

THE ONLY LIMITATION IS THAT WHICH ONE SETS UP IN ONE'S OWN MIND.

TASK 2: CREATE YOUR VISION BOARD

> Images which inspire and trigger emotional response are powerful symbols which directly communicate to the subconscious mind. This is of key importance as a mechanism to bypasses the conscious, critical, analytical mind which often is a detriment to forward momentum.
>
> Images trigger thoughts. Thought impulses are forms of energy. The universe consists of two elements – matter and energy. Through the combination of energy and matter has been created everything which we can perceive, form the largest star which floats in the heavens down to and including ourselves.
>
> Begin at once to put your imagination to work on building a plan or plans to transform your DESIRE into money. Creating your plan visually and putting it into writing will give concrete form to your intangible desires.

First: *Gather images from magazines, news articles, journals, photos and/or print from online that represent who you want to be, what you want to do, what you want to have and where you want to go.*

Second: *Cut out the images which turn you on; those that most excite and inspire you - those that most align with what you desire.*

Third: *Notice the feelings that show up within you at the sight of the images you choose before adhering them to your board. When making your selection, be sure to include pictures that represent not only the assets you'd like to acquire; include images which represent who you are becoming – the qualities and the feelings of the person you are seeking to become.*

Fourth: *Adhere the selected words and images in place.*

Fifth: *Read your Statement of Desire twice daily and as you speak it aloud, look to your Vision Board. Feel the emotions the images cultivate within your subconscious mind.*

IT IS NOT NECESSARY TO REASON HOW YOUR DREAMS WILL BECOME YOUR REALITY. YOUR IMAGINATION WILL CREATE PRACTICAL PLANS THROUGH TRANSMUTATION OF YOUR DESIRE. IMAGINE YOURSELF LIVING THE YOUR VISION NOW.

Paste or draw pictures on these pages, or create a Vision Board outside of the Workbook

FORMS OF IMAGINATION

The imaginative faculty functions in two forms. One is known as Synthetic Imagination and the other as Creative Imagination.

SYNTHETIC IMAGINATION

Through this faculty, one can arrange old concepts, ideas or plans into new combinations. This faculty creates nothing. It merely works with the material of experience, education, and observation with which it is fed. It is the faculty most used by the inventor – with the exception of the genius who draws upon the Creative Imagination when unable to solve a problem through Synthetic Imagination.

CREATIVE IMAGINATION

Through the faculty of Creative Imagination, the finite human mind has direct communication with Infinite Intelligence. It is the faculty through which 'hunches' and 'inspirations' are received. It is by this faculty that all basic or new ideas are handed over to us. It is through this faculty that 'thought vibrations' or 'influences' from the minds of others are received. It is through this faculty that one individual may 'tune-in' or communicate with the subconscious minds of others.

The Creative Imagination works automatically in the manner described in subsequent pages. This faculty functions only when the conscious mind is functioning at an exceedingly high level of 'intensity' or 'energy', as for example when the conscious mind is stimulated through the emotion of a strong desire.

The Creative Imagination becomes more alert, more receptive to influences from the sources mentioned, in proportion to its development through USE. This statement is significant! Ponder over it before moving on.

Both the synthetic and creative faculties of imagination become more alert with use, just as any muscle or organ of the body develops through use.

6

The Sixth Step Towards Riches

ORGANIZED PLANNING

The Crystallization of Desire into Action

> Organized planning is the crystallization of desire into action. You have learned that everything that is created or acquired begins in the form of desire, that desire is taken on the first lap of its journey, from the abstract to the concrete, into the workshop of the imagination, where plans for its transition are created and organized.

MASTERMIND ALLIANCE

You have learned that everything man creates or acquires, begins in the form of DESIRE. That desire is taken on the first lap of its journey from the abstract to the concrete, into the workshop of the IMAGINATION, where PLANS for its transition are created and organized.

1. Ally yourself with a group of as many people as you may need for the creation, and carrying out of your plan, or plans for the accumulation of money-making use of the 'Mastermind' principle described in a later chapter. (Compliance with this instruction is absolutely essential. Do not neglect it.)

2. Before forming your 'Mastermind' alliance, decide what advantages, and benefits, you may offer the individual members of your group, in return for their cooperation. No one will work indefinitely without some form of compensation. No intelligent person will either request or expect another to work without adequate compensation, although this may not always be in the form of money.

3. Arrange to meet with the members of your 'Mastermind' group at least twice a week, and more often if possible, until you have jointly perfected the necessary plan, or plans for the accumulation of money.

4. Maintain PERFECT HARMONY between yourself and every member of your 'Mastermind' group. If you fail to carry out this instruction to the letter, you may expect to meet with failure. The 'Mastermind' principle cannot obtain where PERFECT HARMONY does not prevail.

TASK 1: CREATE YOUR 'MASTERMIND' GROUP

List those whom you would like to participate in your 'Mastermind' group. When selecting potential candidates consider what variety of skills will be required to contribute to the achievement of your success.

Contact Name: _____ From: _____
Email: _____ Phone: _____
Success Qualities: _____
_____
_____

Contact Name: _____ From: _____
Email: _____ Phone: _____
Success Qualities: _____
_____
_____

Contact Name: _____ From: _____
Email: _____ Phone: _____
Success Qualities: _____
_____
_____

Contact Name: _____ From: _____
Email: _____ Phone: _____
Success Qualities: _____
_____
_____

Contact Name: _____ From: _____
Email: _____ Phone: _____
Success Qualities: _____
_____
_____

THE PROCESS OF PLANNING

In chapter two, you were instructed to take six definite, practical steps, as your first move in translating the desire for money into its monetary equivalent. One of these steps is the formation of a DEFINITE practical plan, or plans, through which this transformation may be made.

A group of brains coordinated (or connected) in a spirit of harmony will provide more thought-energy than a single brain, just as a group of electric batteries will provide more energy than a single battery.

No individual person has to themselves, the necessary sum of experience, education, skill, talent, time or knowledge to assure the intended accumulation of wealth without the cooperation of other people.

TASK 2: SCHEDULE TIME WITH YOUR MASTERMIND ALLIANCE

First: Share your intention to create a Mastermind group with your candidates.

Second: Gain confirmation of participation from Mastermind team members.

Third: Schedule time to meet / speak with your Mastermind team bi-weekly.

Fourth: Write down the intended goal and verify the team is aligned in harmony.

Fifth: Plan your work, and work your plan.

TEMPORARY DEFEATS

Henry Ford met with temporary defeat, not only at the beginning of his auto-mobile career, but after he had gone far to the top. He created new plans, and went marching on to financial victory.

James J. Hill met with temporary defeat when he first endeavored to raise the necessary capital to build a railroad from the East to the West, but he, too, turned defeat into victory through new plans.

Thomas A. Edison "failed" ten thousand times before he perfected the incandescent electric light bulb.

We see men who have accumulated great fortunes, but we often recognize only their triumph, overlooking the temporary defeats with they had to surmount before "arriving."

Edison met with temporary defeat ten thousand times before his efforts were crowned successful.

No follower of this philosophy can reasonably expect to accumulate a fortune without experiencing temporary defeat. When defeat comes, accept it as a signal that your plans are not sound, rebuild those plans, and set sail once more toward your coveted goal.

SUCCESS AFFIRMATION

> # A QUITTER NEVER WINS & A WINNER NEVER QUITS!

Make a copy of the above box declaration, then cut it out and place it where you will see it every night before you go to sleep and every morning before you go to work.

No man is ever whipped, until he quits in his own mind.

IF THE FIRST PLAN WHICH YOU ADOPT DOES NOT WORK SUCCESSFULLY, REPLACE IT WITH A NEW PLAN. IF THIS NEW PLAN FAILS TO WORK, REPLACE IT IN TURN WITH STILL ANOTHER, AND SO ON, UNTIL YOU FIND A PLAN WHICH DOES WORK. FAIL FORWARD!

QUALITY – QUANTITY – SPIRIT

QQS FORMULA

The causes of success in marketing services EFFECTIVELY and permanently, have been clearly described. Unless those causes are studied, analyzed, understood and APPLIED, no man can market his services effectively and permanently. Every individual must be their own salesperson of personal services. The QUALITY and the QUANTITY of service rendered, and the SPIRIT in which it is rendered, determine to a large extent, the price, and the duration of employment. To market personal services effectively, (which means a permanent market, at a satisfactory price, under pleasant conditions), one must adopt and follow the "QQS" formula which means that QUALITY, plus QUANTITY, plus the proper SPIRIT of cooperation, equals perfect salesmanship of service. Remember the "QQS" formula, but do more – APPLY IT AS A **HABIT!**

1. **QUALITY** of service shall be construed to mean the performance of every detail, in connection with your position, in the most efficient manner possible, with the object of greater efficiency always in mind.

2. **QUANTITY** of service shall be understood to mean the HABIT of rendering all the service of which you are capable, at all times, with the purpose of increasing the amount of service rendered as greater skill is developed through practice and experience.

3. **SPIRIT** of service shall be construed to mean the HABIT of agreeable, harmonious conduct which will induce cooperation from associates and fellow employees.

The importance of a pleasing personality has been stressed because it is a factor which enables one to render service in the proper SPIRIT. If one has a personality which PLEASES and renders service in a spirit of HARMONY, these assets often make up for deficiencies in both the QUALITY and/or QUANTITY of the service one renders.

NOTHING, HOWEVER, CAN BE SUCCESSFULLY SUBSTITUTED FOR PLEASING CONDUCT.

TASK 3: DETERMINE YOUR QQS RATING

*1. **QUALITY** of service shall be construed to mean the performance of every detail, in connection with your position, in the most efficient manner possible, with the object of greater efficiency always in mind.*

HOW would you rate the quality of service you have delivered, wherever you may have been in service throughout your employment history (to clients, customers, employers and/or as a volunteer)?

_____
_____
_____

*2. **QUANTITY** of service shall be understood to mean the HABIT of rendering all the service of which you are capable, at all times, with the purpose of increasing the amount of service rendered as greater skill is developed through practice and experience. Emphasis is again placed on the word HABIT.*

HAVE I done the minimum required of me, what I was asked to do, only what I was paid for, or have I gone above and beyond?

_____
_____
_____

WHAT could I have done better, improved upon or contributed further to?

_____
_____
_____

*3. **SPIRIT** of service shall be construed to mean the HABIT of agreeable, harmonious conduct which will induce cooperation from associates and fellow employees.*

WERE my work relationships all harmonious or could they have been more agreeable?

_____
_____
_____

THE MAJOR ATTRIBUTES OF LEADERSHIP

1. **Unwavering Courage** based upon knowledge of self, and of one's occupation. No follower wishes to be dominated by a leader who lacks self-confidence and courage. No intelligent follower will be dominated by such a leader very long.

2. **Self-Control.** The man who cannot control himself, can never control others. Self-control sets a mighty example for one's followers, which the more intelligent will emulate.

3. **A keen sense of judgement.** Without a sense of fairness and justice, no leader can command and retain the respect of his followers.

4. **Definiteness of decision.** The man who wavers in his decisions, shows that he is not sure of himself. He cannot lead others successfully.

5. **Definiteness of plans.** The successful leader must plan his work, and work his plan. A leader who moves by guesswork, without practical, definite plans, is comparable to a ship without a rudder. Sooner or later he will land on the rocks.

6. **The habit of doing more than paid for.** One of the penalties of leadership is the necessity of willingness, upon the part of the leader, to do more than he requires of his followers.

7. **A pleasing personality.** No slovenly, careless person can become a successful leader. Leadership calls for respect. Followers will not respect a leader who does not grade high on all of the factors of a Pleasing Personality.

8. **Sympathy and understanding.** The successful leader must be in sympathy with his followers. Moreover, he must understand them and their problems.

9. **Mastery of detail.** Successful leadership calls for mastery of details of the leader's position.

10. **Willingness to assume full responsibility.** The successful leader must be willing to assume responsibility for the mistakes and the shortcomings of his followers. If he tries to shift this responsibility, he will not remain the leader. If one of his followers makes a mistake, and shows himself incompetent, the leader must consider that it is he who failed.

11. **Cooperation.** Successful leaders must understand and apply the principal of cooperative effort and be able to induce their followers to do the same. Leadership calls for POWER and power calls for cooperation.

TASK 4-A: DETERMINE IF YOU ARE A LEADER OR A FOLLOWER

Broadly speaking, there are two types of people in the world. One type is known as LEADERS, and the other as FOLLOWERS. Decide at the outset whether you intend to become a leader in your chosen calling, or remain a follower. The difference in compensation is vast. The follower cannot reasonably expect the compensation to which a leader is entitled, although many followers make the mistake of expecting such pay.

Look to each of the Major Attributes of Leadership as listed. Explain how it is or is not an attribute you convey; include an example to support your claim.

1. _____

2. _____

3. _____

4. _____

5. _____

6. _____

7. _____

8. _____

9. _____

10. _____

11. _____

THE 10 MAJOR CAUSES OF FAILURE IN LEADERSHIP

1. **Inability to organize details.** Efficient leadership calls for ability to organize and to master details. No genuine leader is ever 'too busy' to do anything which may be required of him in his capacity as a leader.

2. **Unwillingness to render humble service.** Truly great leaders are willing, when occasion demands, to perform any sort of labor which they would ask another to perform.

3. **Expectation of pay for what they 'know' instead of what they do with that which they know.** The world does not pay men for that which they 'know'. It pays them for what they DO, or induce others to do.

4. **Fear of competition from followers.** The leader who fears that one of his followers may take his position is practically sure to realize that fear sooner or later. The able leader trains understudies to whom he may delegate, at will, any of the details of his position. Only in this way may a leader multiply himself and prepare himself to be at many places, and give attention to many things at one time.

5. **Lack of imagination.** Without imagination, the leader is incapable of meeting emergencies, and of creating plans by which to guide his followers efficiently.

6. **Selfishness.** The leader who claims all the honor for the work of his followers, is sure to be met by resentment. The really great leader CLAIMS NONE OF THE HONORS. He is contented to see the honors, when there are any, go to his followers, because he knows that most men will work harder for commendation and recognition then they will for money alone.

7. **Intemperance.** Followers do not respect an intemperate leader. Moreover, intemperance in any of its various forms, destroys the endurance and the vitality of all who indulge in it.

8. **Disloyalty.** The leader who is not loyal to his trust, and to his associates, those above him, and those below him, cannot long maintain his leadership. Disloyalty marks one as being less than the dust of the earth, and brings down on one's head the contempt he deserves. Lack of loyalty is one of the major causes of failure in every walk of life.

9. **Emphasis on the 'authority' of leadership.** The efficient leader leads by encouraging, and not by trying to instill fear in the hearts of his followers. The leader who tries to impress his followers with his "authority" comes within the category of leadership through FORCE. If a leader is a REAL LEADER, he will have no need to advertise that fact except by his conduct.

10. **Emphasis of title.** The competent leader requires no 'title' to give him the respect of his followers. The man who makes too much over his title generally has little else to emphasize.

TASK 4-B: DETERMINE IF YOU ARE A LEADER OR A FOLLOWER

It is no disgrace to be a follower. On the other hand, it is no credit to remain a follower. Most great leaders began in the capacity of followers. They became great leaders because they were INTELLIGENT FOLLOWERS. With few exceptions, the man who cannot follow a leader intelligently, cannot become an efficient leader. The man who can follow a leader most efficiently, is usually the man who develops into leadership most rapidly. An intelligent follower has many advantages, among them the opportunity to acquire knowledge from their leader.

Look to each of the Major Cause of Failure as listed. Explain how it is or is not an attribute you convey; include an example to support your claim.

1. _____
2. _____
3. _____
4. _____
5. _____
6. _____
7. _____
8. _____
9. _____
10. _____

TASK 5: TAKE INVENTORY OF FAILURES

There are thirty major reasons for failure, and thirteen major principles through which people accumulate fortunes. A description of the thirty major causes of failure will be given. As you go over the list, check yourself by it, point by point for the purpose of discovering how many of these causes-of-failure have stood between you and success.

- ☐ **UNFAVORABLE HEREDITARY BACKGROUND.** There is but little, if anything, which can be done for people who are born with a deficiency in brain power. This philosophy offers but one method of bridging this weakness through the aid of the Mastermind. Observe with profit, however, that this is only one of the 30 causes of failure which may not be easily corrected by any individual.

- ☐ **LACK OF A WELL-DEFINED PURPOSE IN LIFE.** There is no hope of success for the person who does not have a central purpose, or definite goal at which to aim. Ninety-eight out of every hundred of those whom I have analyzed had no such aim. Perhaps this was the major cause of their failure.

- ☐ **LACK OF AMBITION TO AIM ABOVE MEDIOCRITY.** We offer no hope for the person who is so indifferent as not to want to get ahead in life, and who is not willing to pay the price.

- ☐ **INSUFFICIENT EDUCATION.** This is a handicap which may be overcome with comparative ease. Experience has proven that the best-educated people are often those who are known as 'self-made' or self-educated. It takes more than a college degree to make one a person of learned to get whatever he or she wants in life without violating the rights of others. Education consists not so much of knowledge, but of knowledge effectively and persistently applied. People are paid not merely for what they know, but more particularly for what they do with that which they know.

- ☐ **LACK OF SELF-DISCIPLINE.** Discipline comes through self-control. This means that one must control all negative qualities. Before you can control conditions, you must first control yourself. Self-mastery is the hardest job you will ever tackle. If you do not conquer self, you will be conquered by self. You may see at one and the same time both your best friend and your greatest enemy, by stepping in front of a mirror.

- **ILL HEALTH.** No person may enjoy outstanding success without good health. Many of the causes of ill health are subject to mastery and control. These are the primary factors:
  a. Overeating of foods not conducive to health
  b. Wrong habits of thought; giving expression to negatives
  c. Wrong use of, and over indulgence in sex
  d. Lack of proper physical exercise
  e. An inadequate supply of fresh air, due to improper breathing

- **UNFAVORABLE ENVIRONMENTAL INFLUENCES DURING CHILDHOOD.** 'As the twig is bent, so shall the tree grow.' Most people who have criminal tendencies acquire them as the result of bad environment and improper associates during childhood.

- **PROCRASTINATION.** This is one of the most common causes of failure. 'Old Man Procrastination' stands within the shadow of every human being, waiting his opportunity to spoil one's chances of success. Most of us go through life as failures, because we are waiting for the "time to be right" to start doing something worthwhile. Do not wait. The time will never be "just right." Start where you stand, and work with whatever tools you may have at your command, and better tools will be found as you go along.

- **LACK OF PERSISTENCE.** Most of us are good "starters" but poor "finishers" of everything we begin. Moreover, people are prone to give up at the first signs of defeat. There is no substitute for PERSISTENCE. The person who makes PERSISTENCE his watch-word, discovers that 'Old Man Failure' finally becomes tired, and makes his departure. Failure cannot cope with PERSISTENCE.

- **NEGATIVE PERSONALITY.** There is no hope of success for the person who repels people through a negative personality. Success comes through the application of POWER, and power is attained through the cooperative efforts of other people. A negative personality will not induce cooperation.

- **LACK OF CONTROLLED SEXUAL URGE.** Sex energy is the most powerful of all the stimuli which move people into ACTION. Because it is the most powerful of the emotions, it must be controlled, through transmutation, and converted into other channels.

- **UNCONTROLLED DESIRE FOR 'SOMETHING FOR NOTHING.'** The gambling instinct drives millions of people to failure. Evidence of this may be found in a study of the Wall Street crash of 1929, during which millions of people tried to make money by gambling on stock margins.

- **LACK OF CONCENTRATION OF EFFORT.** The 'jack-of-all-trades' seldom is good at any. Concentrate all of your efforts on one DEFINITE CHIEF AIM.

- ☐ **LACK OF A WELL-DEFINED POWER OF DECISION.** Men who succeed reach decisions promptly, and change them, if at all, very slowly. Men who fail, reach decisions, if at all, very slowly, and change them frequently, and quickly. Indecision and procrastination are twin brothers. Where one is found, the other may usually be found also. Kill off this pair before they completely 'hog-tie' you to the treadmill of FAILURE.

- ☐ **ONE OR MORE OF THE SIX BASIC FEARS.** These fears have been analyzed for you in a later chapter. They must be mastered before you can market your services effectively.

- ☐ **WRONG SELECTION OF A MATE IN MARRIAGE.** This a most common cause of failure. The relationship of marriage brings people intimately into contact. Unless this relationship is harmonious, failure is likely to follow. Moreover, it will be a form of failure that is marked by misery and unhappiness, destroying all signs of AMBITION.

- ☐ **OVER-CAUTION.** The person who takes no chances, generally has to take whatever is left when others are through choosing. Over-caution is as bad as under-caution. Both are extremes to be guarded against. Life itself is filled with the element of chance.

- ☐ **WRONG SELECTION OF ASSOCIATES IN BUSINESS.** This is one of the most common causes of failure in business. In marketing personal services, one should use great care to select an employer who will be an inspiration, and who is, himself, intelligent and successful. We emulate those with whom we associate most closely. Pick an employer who is worth emulating.

- ☐ **SUPERSTITION AND PREJUDICE.** Superstition is a form of fear. It is also a sign of ignorance. Men who succeed keep open minds and are afraid of nothing.

- ☐ **WRONG SELECTION OF A VOCATION.** No man can succeed in a line of endeavor which he does not like. The most essential step in the marketing of personal services is that of selecting an occupation into which you can throw yourself wholeheartedly.

- ☐ **THE HABIT OF INDISCRIMINATE SPENDING.** The spend-thrift cannot succeed, mainly because he stands eternally in FEAR OF POVERTY. Form the habit of systematic saving by putting aside a definite percentage of your income. Money in the bank gives one a very safe foundation of COURAGE when bargaining for the sale of personal services. Without money, one must take what one is offered, and be glad to get it.

- ☐ **LACK OF ENTHUSIASM.** Without enthusiasm one cannot be convincing. Moreover, enthusiasm is contagious, and the person who has it under control, is generally welcome in any group of people.

- ☐ **INTOLERANCE.** The person with a 'closed' mind on any subject seldom gets ahead. Intolerance means that one has stopped acquiring knowledge. The most damaging forms of intolerance are those connected with religious, racial, and political differences of opinion.

- ☐ **INTEMPERANCE.** The most damaging forms of intemperance are connected with eating, strong drink, and sexual activities. Overindulgence in any of these is fatal to success.

- ☐ **INABILITY TO COOPERATE WITH OTHERS.** More people lose their positions and their big opportunities in life, because of this fault, than for all other reasons combined. It is a fault which no well-informed business man, or leader will tolerate.

- ☐ **POSSESSION OF POWER THAT WAS NOT ACQUIRED THROUGH SELF EFFORT.** (Sons and daughters of wealthy people and others who inherit money which they did not earn). Power in the hands of one who did not acquire it gradually, is often fatal to success. QUICK RICHES are more dangerous than poverty.

- ☐ **INTENTIONAL DISHONESTY.** There is no substitute for honesty. One may be temporarily dishonest by force of circumstances over which one has no control, without permanent damage. But there is NO HOPE for the person who is dishonest by choice. Sooner or later, his deeds will catch up with him, and he will pay by loss of reputation, and perhaps even loss of liberty.

- ☐ **EGOTISM AND VANITY.** These qualities serve as red lights which warn others to keep away. THEY ARE FATAL TO SUCCESS.

- ☐ **GUESSING INSTEAD OF THINKING.** Most people are too indifferent or lazy to acquire FACTS with which to THINK ACCURATELY. They prefer to act on 'opinions' created by guesswork or snap-judgements.

- ☐ **LACK OF CAPITAL.** This is a common cause of failure among those who start out in business for the first time, without sufficient reserve of capital to absorb the shock of their mistakes, and to carry them over until they have established a REPUTATION.

It is one thing to want money
- everyone wants more -
but it is something entirely different
to be worth more! Many people mistake
their wants for their just dues.

Your financial requirements or wants have
nothing whatever to do with your worth.
Your value is established entirely by your
ability to render useful service or your
capacity to induce others to
render such service.

TASK 6: SELF INVENTORY

Self-Analysis Questionnaire for Personal Inventory

1. Have I attained the goal which I established as my objective for this year? (You should work with a definite yearly objective to be attained as a part of your major life objective).
___
___
___
___

2. Have I delivered service of the best possible QUALITY of which I was capable, or could I have improved any part of this service?
___
___
___
___

3. Have I delivered service in the greatest possible QUANTITY of which I was capable?
___
___
___
___

4. Has the spirit of my conduct been harmonious and cooperative at all times?
___
___
___
___

5. Have I permitted the habit of PROCRASTINATION to decrease my efficiency and if so, to what extent?
___
___
___
___

6. Have I improved my personality, and if so, in what ways?

_____
_____
_____
_____

7. Have I been PERSISTENT in following my plans through to completion?

_____
_____
_____
_____

8. Have I reached DECISIONS PROMPTLY and DEFINITELY on all occasions?

_____
_____
_____
_____

9. Have I permitted any one or more of the six basic fears to decrease my efficiency?

_____
_____
_____
_____

10. Have I been either "over-cautious," or "under-cautious?"

_____
_____
_____
_____

11. Has my relationship with my associates in work been pleasant, or unpleasant? If it has been unpleasant, has the fault been partly, or wholly mine?

_____
_____
_____
_____

12. Have I dissipated any of my energy through lack of CONCENTRATION of effort?

13. Have I been open minded and tolerant in connection with all subjects?

14. In what way have I improved my ability to render service?

15. Have I been intemperate in any of my habits?

16. Have I expressed, either openly or secretly, any form of EGOTISM?

17. Has my conduct toward my associates been such that it has induced them to respect me?

18. Have my opinions and DECISIONS been based upon guesswork, or accuracy of analysis and thought?
___
___
___
___

19. Have I followed the habit of budgeting my time, my expenses, and my income and have I been conservative in these budgets?
___
___
___
___

20. How much time have I devoted to unprofitable effort which I might have used to better advantage?
___
___
___
___

21. How may I re-budget my time, and change my habits so I will be more efficient during the coming year?
___
___
___
___

22. Have I been guilty of any conduct which was not approved by my conscience?
___
___
___
___

23. In what ways have I rendered more service and better service than I was paid to render?
___
___
___

24. Have I been unfair to anyone, and if so, in what way?

25. If I had been the purchaser of my own services for the year, would I be satisfied with my purchase?

26. Am I in the right vocation, and if not, why not?

27. Has the purchaser of my services been satisfied with the service I have rendered, and if not, why not?

28. What is my present rating on the fundamental principles of success? (Make this rating fairly and frankly, and have it checked by someone who is outrageous enough to do it accurately).

Definiteness of Decision

One of Henry Ford's most outstanding qualities is his habit of reaching decisions quickly and definitely, and changing them slowly. This quality is so pronounced in Mr. Ford that it has given him the reputation of being obstinate. It was this quality which prompted Mr. Ford to continue to manufacture his famous Model "T" (the worlds ugliest car), when all of his advisors, and many of the purchasers of the car, were urging him to change it.

Perhaps Mr. Ford delayed too long in making the changes, but the other side of the story is that Mr. Ford's firmness of decision yielded a huge fortune, before the change in model became necessary. There is but little doubt that Mr. Ford's habit of definiteness of decision assumes the proportion of obstinacy but this quality is preferable to slowness in reaching decisions and quickness in changing them.

7

The Seventh Step Towards Riches

DECISION

The Master of Procrastination

> Accurate analysis of over 25,000 men and women who had experienced failure, disclosed the fact that lack of decision was near the head of the list of the 30 major causes of failure. this is no mere statement of a theory - it is a fact.
>
> Analysis of several hundred people who had accumulated fortunes well beyond the million-dollar mark disclosed the fact that every one of them had the habit of reaching decisions promptly and of changing these decisions slowly, if, and when they were changed. People who fail to accumulate money, without exception, have the habit of reaching decisions, if at all, very slowly, and of changing these decisions quickly and often.

TASK 1: DECISION SELF ANALYSIS

> *Keep your own counsel when you begin to put into practice the principles described in this book by reaching your own decisions and following them. Take no one into your confidence except the members of your Mastermind Alliance, and be very sure in your section of this group that you choose ONLY those who will be in COMPLETE SYMPATHY and HARMONY with YOUR PURPOSE.*
>
> *Close friends and relatives, while not meaning to do so, often handicap one through opinions and sometimes through ridicule, which is meant to be humorous. Thousands of men and women carry inferiority complexes with them all through life because some well-meaning, but ignorant person destroyed their confidence through opinions or ridicule.*

List comments or occasions when you had shared your thoughts, dreams or ambitions and had been met with opposing opinions, ridicule, fear and doubt.

_____
_____
_____
_____
_____
_____

How had those experiences affected your feelings?

_____
_____
_____
_____
_____

How had those experiences impacted your desire to take action?

_____
_____
_____
_____
_____

TASK 2: MAKE DECISIONS THAT SERVE YOUR DEFINITE CHIEF AIM

The majority of people who fail to accumulate money sufficient for their needs are generally, easily influenced by the 'opinions' of others. They permit the news, social media, gossiping friends, neighbors or colleagues, to do their 'thinking' for them. Opinions are the cheapest commodities on earth. Everyone has a flock of opinions ready to be wised upon anyone who will accept them. If you are influenced by opinions when you reach decisions, you will not succeed in any under-training, much less in that transmuting your own desire into money. If you are influenced by the opinions of others, you will have no desire of your own.

You have a brain and mind of your own. Use it, and reach your own decisions. If you need factors or information from other people, to enable you to reach decisions, as you probably will in many instances, acquire these facts or secure the information you need quietly, without disclosing your purpose.

What are three decisions you can make with confidence right now?

1. _____
_____

2. _____
_____

3. _____
_____

What are three decisions you get to make personally or professionally to bring you closer to your goals and/or dreams?

1. _____
_____

2. _____
_____

3. _____
_____

DEEDS AND NOT WORDS

Let one of your first decisions be to keep a closed mouth and open ears and eyes.

As a reminder to yourself to follow this advice, it will be helpful if you copy the following epigram in large letters and place it where you will see it daily.

TELL THE WORLD WHAT YOU INTEND TO DO, BUT FIRST SHOW IT.

REMEMBER THAT EVERY TIME YOU OPEN YOUR MOUTH IN THE PRESENCE OF A PERSON WHO HAS AN ABUNDANCE OF KNOWLEDGE, YOU DISPLAY TO THAT PERSON YOUR EXACT STOCK OF KNOWLEDGE, OR YOUR LACK OF IT! GENUINE WISDOM IS USUALLY CONSPICUOUS THROUGH MODESTY AND SILENCE.

FREEDOM OR DEATH ON A DECISION

The value of decisions depends upon the courage required to render them. The great decisions, which served as the foundation of civilization, were reached assuming great risks, which often meant the possibility of death.

Lincoln's decision to use his famous Proclamation of Emancipation, which gave freedom to the colored people of America, was rendered with full understanding that his act would turn thousands of friends and political supporters against him. He knew, too, that the carrying out of the proclamation would mean death to thousands of men on the battlefield; in the end, it cost Lincoln his life. That required courage.

Socrates' decision to drink the cup of poison, rather than compromise in his personal belief, was a decision of courage. It turned time ahead a thousand years, and age to people then unborn, the right to freedom of thought and of speech.

The decision of General Robert E. Lee, when he came to the parting of the ways with the Union, and took up the cause of the South, was a decision of courage. He well knew that it might cost him his own life, and that it would surely cost the lives of others.

But the greatest decision of all time, as far as any American citizen is concerned, was reached in Philadelphia, July 4, 1776, when fifty-six men signed their names to a document, which they well knew would bring freedom to all Americans, or leave every one of the fifty-six hanging from the gallows!

8

The Eight Step Towards Riches

PERSISTENCE

The Sustained Effort Necessary to induce Faith

> Persistence is an essential factor in the procedure of transmuting desire into its monetary equivalent. The basis of persistence is the power of will.

TASK 1: TESTING YOUR PERSISTENCE

If you are following this book with the intention of applying the knowledge it conveys, your first test as to your PERSISTENCE will come when you begin to follow the six steps described in the second chapter. Unless you are one of the two out of every hundred who already have a DEFINITE GOAL at which you are aiming and a DEFINITE PLAN for its attainment, you may read the instructions, and then pass on with your daily routine, and never comply with those instructions.

The author is checking you up at this point, because lack of persistence is one of the major causes of failure. Moreover, experience with thousands of people has proved that lack of persistence is a weakness common to the majority of men. It is a weakness which may be overcome by effort. The ease with which lack of persistence may be conquered will depend entirely upon the INTENSITY OF ONE'S DESIRE.

The starting point of all achievement is DESIRE. Keep this constantly in mind. Weak desires bring weak results, just as a small amount of fire makes a small amount of heat. If you find yourself lacking in persistence, this weakness may be remedied by building a stronger fire under your desires.

<u>Look back to Task 6 of Chapter 1 and begin immediately to carry out the instructions given in connection with the six steps.</u>

The eagerness with which you follow these instructions is an indicator of how much or how little you desire to accumulate wealth. If you find that you are indifferent, you may be sure that you have not yet acquired the 'money consciousness' which you must possess before you can be sure of accumulating a fortune.

EVERY FAILURE BRINGS WITH IT THE SEED OF AN EQUIVALENT SUCCESS.

DEFINITE CAUSES OF PERSISTENCE

- **DEFINITENESS OF PURPOSE.** Knowing what one wants is the first and, perhaps, the most important step toward the development of persistence. A strong motive forces one to surmount many difficulties.

- **DESIRE.** It is comparatively easy to acquire and to maintain persistence in pursuing the object of intense desire.

- **SELF-RELIANCE.** Belief in one's ability to carry out a plan encourages one to follow the plan through with persistence. (Self-reliance can be developed through the principle described in the chapter on autosuggestion).

- **DEFINITENESS OF PLANS.** Organized plans, even though they may be weak and entirely impractical, encourage persistence.

- **ACCURATE KNOWLEDGE.** Knowing that one's plans are sound, based upon experience or observation, encourages persistence; 'guessing' instead of 'knowing' destroys persistence.

- **COOPERATION.** Sympathy, understanding, and harmonious cooperation with others tend to develop persistence.

- **WILL-POWER.** The habit of concentrating one's thoughts upon the building of plans for the attainment of a definite purpose, leads to persistence.

- **HABIT.** Persistence is the direct result of habit. The mind absorbs and becomes a part of the daily experiences upon which it feeds. Fear, the worst of all enemies, can be effectively cured by forced repetition of acts of courage. Everyone who has seen active service in war knows this.

TASK 2: SELF ANALYSIS
SYMPTOMS OF LACK OF PERSISTENCE

Take inventory of yourself, and determine in what particularly way, if any, you are lacking in this essential quality. Measure yourself courageously, point by point, and see how many of the factors of persistence you lack. The analysis may lead to discoveries that will give you a new grip on yourself.

- ☐ Failure to recognize and to clearly define exactly what one wants.
- ☐ Procrastination, with or without cause. (Usually backed up with a formidable array of alibis and excuses).
- ☐ Lack of interest in acquiring specialized knowledge.
- ☐ Indecision, the habit of "passing the buck" on all occasions, instead of facing issues squarely. (Also backed by alibis).
- ☐ The habit of relying upon alibis instead of creating definite plans for the solution of problems.
- ☐ Self-satisfaction. There is but little remedy for this affliction, and no hope for those who suffer from it.
- ☐ Indifference, usually reflected in one's readiness to compromise on all occasions, rather than meet opposition and fight it.
- ☐ The habit of blaming others for one's mistakes, and accepting unfavorable circumstances as being unavoidable.
- ☐ Weakness of desire, due to neglect in the choice of motives that impel action.
- ☐ Willingness, even eagerness, to quit at the first sign of defeat. (Based upon one or more of the 6 basic fears).
- ☐ Lack of organized plans, placed in writing where they may be analyzed.
- ☐ The habit of neglecting to move on ideas, or to grasp opportunity when it presents itself. Wishing instead of willing.
- ☐ The habit of compromising with POVERTY instead of aiming at riches. General absence of ambition to be, to do, and to own.
- ☐ Searching for all the short-cuts to riches, trying to get without giving a fair equivalent, usually reflected in the habit of gambling, endeavoring to drive 'sharp' bargains.
- ☐ Fear of criticism, failure to create plans and to put them into action, because of what other people will think, do, or say. This enemy belongs at the head of the list, because it generally exists in one's subconscious mind, where its presence is not recognized. (See the Six Basic Fears in a later chapter).

The Fear of Criticism

"When Andrew Carnegie suggested that I decide twenty years to the organization of a philosophy of individual achievement my first impulse of thought was fear of what people might say. The suggestion set up a goal for me, far out of proportion to any I had ever conceived. As quick as a flash, my mind began to create alibis and excuses, all of them traceable to the inherent fear of criticism. Something inside of me said, 'You can't do it - the job is too big and requires too much time - what will your relatives think of you? - how will you earn a living? - no one has ever organized a philosophy of success, what right have you to believe you can do it? - who are you, anyway, to aim so high? - remember your humble birth - what do you know about philosophy - people will think you are crazy - (and they did) - why hasn't some other person done this before now?'

These, and many other questions flashed into my mind, and demanded attention. It seemed as if the whole world had suddenly turned its attention to me with the purpose of ridiculing me into giving up all desire to carry out Mr. Carnegie's suggestion.

I had a fine opportunity, then and there, to kill off ambition before it gained control of me. Later in life, after having analyzed thousands of people, I discovered that most ideas are stillborn, and need the breath of life injected into them through definite plans of immediate action. The time to nurse an idea is at the time of its birth. Every minute it lives gives it a better chance of surviving."

The fear of criticism is at the bottom of the destruction of most ideas which never reached the planning and action stage.

TASK 3: PRACTICE DEVELOPING PERSISTENCE

There are four simple steps which lead to the habit of persistence. They call for no great amount of intelligence, no particular amount of education, and but little time or effort. The necessary steps are:

1. A definite purposed backed by burning desire for its fulfillment.

My definite purpose is:

_____
_____
_____

2. A definite plan, expressed in continuous action.

My definite plan is:

_____
_____
_____

3. A mind closed tightly against all negative and discouraging influences, including the negative suggestions of relatives, friends, acquaintances, and/or colleagues.

To strengthen and protect my mind I will:

_____
_____
_____

4. A friendly alliance with one or more persons who will encourage one to follow through with both plan and purpose.

The people who encourage me are:

_____
_____
_____

These four steps are essential for success in all walks of life. The entire purpose of the thirteen principles of this philosophy is to enable one to take these four steps as a matter of habit.

REMINDER

There is a magnificent reward for all who learn to take these steps. It is the privilege of writing one's own ticket, and of making Life yield whatever price is asked.

- These are the steps by which one may control one's economic destiny.

- They are the steps that lead to freedom and independence of thought.

- They are the steps that lead to riches, in small or great quantities.

- They lead the way to power, fame, and worldly recognition.

- They are the four steps which guarantee favorable "breaks".

- They are the steps that convert dreams into physical realities.

They lead, also, to the mastery of FEAR, DISCOURAGEMENT, and INDIFFERENCE.

9

The Ninth Step Towards Riches

POWER OF THE MASTERMIND

The Driving Force

TASK 1: NOTICE YOUR EMOTIONAL RESPONSE TO 'POWER'

> ***POWER** is essential for success in the accumulation of money. Plans are inert and useless, without sufficient power to translate them into action. This chapter will describe the method by which an individual may attain and apply power.*
>
> ***POWER** may be defined as 'organized and intelligently directed knowledge'. Power, as the term is here used, refers to organized effort, sufficient to enable an individual to transmute DESIRE into its monetary equivalent. Organized effort is produced through the coordination of effort of two or more people, who work toward a definite end, in a spirit of harmony.*
>
> ***POWER** is required for the accumulation of money! Power is necessary for the retention of money after it has been accumulated!*

Write what you make the word 'Power' mean to you and list the feelings that you experience when reading the above paragraphs.

INTERPRET 'POWER' AS MEANING: I FEEL:

_____   _____
_____   _____
_____   _____
_____   _____
_____   _____
_____   _____

Do those feelings contribute to or are they detrimental to your success and why?

_____
_____
_____
_____
_____
_____
_____

SOURCES OF KNOWLEDGE

- ***INFINITE INTELLIGENCE.*** This source of knowledge may be contacted through the procedure described in another chapter, with the aid of Creative Imagination.

- ***ACCUMULATED EXPERIENCE.*** The accumulated experience of man, (or that portion of it which has been organized and recorded), may be found in any well-equipped public library. An important part of this accumulated experience is taught in public schools and colleges, where it has been classified and organized.

- ***EXPERIMENT AND RESEARCH.*** In the field of science, and in practically every other walk of life, men are gathering, classifying, and organizing new facts daily. This is the source to which one must turn when knowledge is not available through "accumulated experience." Here, too, the Creative Imagination must often be used.

Knowledge may be acquired from any of the foregoing sources. It may be converted into POWER by organizing it into definite PLANS and by expressing those plans in terms of ACTION. Examination of the three major sources of knowledge will readily disclose the difficulty an individual would have, if he depended upon his efforts alone, in assembling knowledge and expressing it through definite plans in terms of ACTION. If his plans are comprehensive, and if they contemplate large proportions, he must, generally, induce others to cooperate with him, before he can inject into them the necessary element of POWER.

GREAT POWER CAN BE ACCUMULATED THROUGH NO OTHER PRINCIPLE THAN THAT OF THE MASTERMIND.

TASK 2: REASSESSING YOUR MASTERMIND

The 'Mastermind' may be defined as: "Coordination of knowledge and effort in a spirit of harmony between two or more people, for the attainment of a definite purpose."

Refer back to your Mastermind list. Place the names of the people who you have chosen to be in your Mastermind group. Add to each name the success benefits they have brought to you to date (I.e., passion, vision, contacts, capital, etc.).

NAME: _____

SUCCESS BENEFIT: _____

NAME: _____

SUCCESS BENEFIT: _____

NAME: _____

SUCCESS BENEFIT: _____

NAME: _____

SUCCESS BENEFIT: _____

NAME: _____

SUCCESS BENEFIT: _____

What qualities that you need in a Mastermind partner are still missing?

_____
_____

Who embodying this quality might be a good addition to your Mastermind group?

_____
_____

10

The Tenth Step Towards Riches

THE MYSTERY OF SEX TRANSMUTATION

The Practice of Energy Exchange

> The meaning of the word "transmute" is, in simple language, "the changing, or transferring of one element, or form of energy, into another."

THE TEN MIND STIMULI

The human mind responds to stimuli, through which it may be "keyed up" to high rates of vibration, known as enthusiasm, creative imagination, intense desire, etc. The stimuli to which the mind responds most freely are:

1. The desire for sex expression
2. Love
3. A burning desire for fame, power, or financial gain, MONEY
4. Music
5. Friendship between either those of the same sex or those of the opposite sex
6. A Mastermind Alliance based upon the harmony of two or more people who ally themselves for spiritual or temporal advancement
7. Mutual suffering such as that experienced by people who are persecuted
8. Autosuggestion
9. Fear
10. Narcotics and alcohol

The desire for sex expression comes at the head of the list of stimuli, which most effectively "step-up" the vibrations of the mind and start the "wheels" of physical action. Eight of these stimuli are natural and constructive. Two are destructive. The list is here presented for the purpose of enabling you to make a comparative study of the major sources of mind stimulation. From this study, it will be readily seen that the emotion of sex is, by great odds, the most intense and powerful of all mind stimuli.

This comparison is necessary as a foundation for proof of the statement that trans- mutation of sex energy may lift one to the status of a genius.

A MIND STIMULANT IS ANY INFLUENCE WHICH WILL EITHER TEMPORARILY, OR PERMANENTLY INCREASE THE VIBRATIONS OF THOUGHT.

TASK 1: NOTICE YOUR MIND STIMULI

> Sex desire is the most powerful of human desires. The emotion of sex has back of it the possibility of three constructive potentialities, they are:
>
> 1. The perpetuation of mankind.
> 2. The maintenance of health, (as a therapeutic agency, it has no equal).
> 3. The transformation of mediocrity into genius through transmutation.
>
> Sex transmutation is simple and easily explained. It means the switching of the mind from thoughts of physical expression, to thoughts of some other nature.

List the stimuli which most prominently affect you.

1. _____
2. _____
3. _____
4. _____
5. _____
6. _____
7. _____
8. _____
9. _____
10. _____

List the most impactful and positive stimuli from the above list and determine a mechanism you can implement to more effectively leverage each.

Stimuli:_____ Strategy: _____

Stimuli:_____ Strategy: _____

Stimuli:_____ Strategy: _____

"GENIUS" IS DEVELOPED THROUGH THE SIXTH SENSE

The reality of a "sixth sense" has been fairly well established. This sixth sense is "Creative Imagination." The faculty of creative imagination is one which the majority of people never use during an entire lifetime, and if used at all, it usually happens by mere accident. A relatively small number of people use, with deliberation and purpose aforethought, the faculty of creative imagination.

Those who use this faculty voluntarily, and with understanding of its functions, are GENII. The faculty of creative imagination is the direct link between the finite mind of man and Infinite Intelligence. All so-called revelations, referred to in the realm of religion, and all discoveries of basic or new principles in the field of invention, take place through the faculty of creative imagination.

TASK 2: THE GIFT OF IDEAS

> When ideas or concepts flash into one's mind, through what is popularly called a "hunch", they come from one or more of the following sources:
>
> Infinite Intelligence
>
> One's subconscious mind, where in is stored every sense impression and thought impulse which ever reached the brain through any of the five senses
>
> From the mind of some other person who has just released the thought, or picture of the idea or concept, through conscious thought, or
>
> From the other person's subconscious store house.
>
> There are no other KNOWN sources from which "inspired" ideas or "hunches" may be received.

List ideas and/or hunches that have spontaneously popped into your mind.

1. _____
2. _____
3. _____
4. _____
5. _____
6. _____
7. _____
8. _____
9. _____
10. _____

THE MERE POSSESSION OF SEX ENERGY ITSELF IS NOT SUFFICIENT TO PRODUCE A GENIUS. THE ENERGY MUST BE TRANSMUTED FROM DESIRE FOR MERELY PHYSICAL CONTACT, INTO SOME OTHER FORM OF DESIRE AND ACTION BEFORE IT WILL LIFT ONE TO THE STATUS OF GENIUS.

SITTING FOR IDEAS

The late Dr. Elmer R. Gates, of Chevy Chase, Maryland, created more than 200 useful patents, many of them basic, through the process of cultivating and using the creative faculty. His method is both significant and interesting to one interested in attaining to the status of genius, in which category Dr. Gates, unquestionably belonged. Dr. Gates was one of the really great, though less publicized scientists of the world.

In his laboratory, he had what he called his "personal communication room." It was practically sound proof, and so arranged that all light could be shut out. It was equipped with a small table, on which he kept a pad of writing paper. In front of the table, on the wall, was an electric pushbutton, which controlled the lights. When Dr. Gates desired to draw upon the forces available to him through his Creative Imagination, he would go into this room, seat himself at the table, shut off the lights, and CONCENTRATE upon the KNOWN factors of the invention on which he was working, remaining in that position until ideas began to "flash" into his mind in connection with the UNKNOWN factors of the invention.

On one occasion, ideas came through so fast that he was forced to write for almost three hours. When the thoughts stopped flowing, and he examined his notes, he found they contained a minute description of principles which had not a parallel among the known data of the scientific world. Moreover, the answer to his problem was intelligently presented in those notes. In this manner Dr. Gates completed over 200 patents, which had been begun, but not completed, by "half-baked" brains. Evidence of the truth of this statement is in the United States Patent Office. Dr. Gates earned his living by "sitting for ideas" for individuals and corporations. Some of the largest corporations in America paid him substantial fees, by the hour, for "sitting for ideas."

TASK 3: YOUR PERSONAL COMMUNICATION ROOM

> The reasoning faculty is often faulty, because it is largely guided by one's accumulated experience. Not all knowledge, which one accumulates through "experience," is accurate. Ideas received through the creative faculty are much more reliable, for the reason that they come from sources more reliable than any which are available to the reasoning faculty of the mind. The major difference between the genius and the ordinary "crank" inventor, may be found in the fact that the genius works through his faculty of creative imagination, while the "crank" knows nothing of this faculty.

Isolate yourself in a private place; a location that is quiet, peaceful and dark. Close your eyes and take a few conscious breaths before settling into a natural breathing pattern. Concentrate on your Statement of Desire or Statement of Purpose and say it to yourself aloud. Then sit in silence. Remain in this position until ideas or images 'flash' into your mind. Write the ideas down no matter how bizarre, whether they appear related or unrelated. Return to this practice consistently and act upon the ideas that resonate with you most.

My ideas:
_____
_____
_____
_____
_____
_____
_____
_____
_____
_____
_____
_____
_____
_____
_____
_____
_____
_____

WHY PEOPLE SELDOM SUCCEED BEFORE FORTY

Hill discovered, from the analysis of over 25,000 people, that men who succeed in an outstanding way, seldom do so before the age of forty and more often they do not strike their real pace until they are well beyond the age of fifty. This fact was so astounding that it prompted him to go into the study of its cause most carefully, carrying the investigation over a period of more than twelve years.

This study disclosed the fact that the major reason why the majority of men who succeed do not begin to do so before the age of forty to fifty, is their tendency to DISSIPATE their energies through over indulgence in physical expression of the emotion of sex. The majority of men never learn that the urge of sex has other possibilities, which far transcend in importance, that of mere physical expression. The majority of those who make this discovery, do so after having wasted many years at a period when the sex energy is at its height, prior to the age of forty-five to fifty. This usually is followed by noteworthy achievement.

TASK 4: INCREASING YOUR PERSONAL MAGNETISM

> The factor of personality known as "personal magnetism" is nothing more nor less than sex energy. Highly sexed people always have a plentiful supply of magnetism. Through cultivation and understanding, this vital force may be drawn upon and used to great advantage in the relationships between people.

Below you will find the various ways this energy may be communicated to others. List how you can increase your own personal magnetism in each area.

1. <u>The handshake.</u> The touch of the hand indicates, instantly, the presence of magnetism, or the lack of it.
_____
_____

2. <u>The tone of voice.</u> Magnetism, or sex energy, is the factor with which the voice may be colored, or made musical and charming.
_____
_____

3. <u>Posture and carriage of the body.</u> Highly sexed people move briskly, and with grace and ease.
_____
_____

4. <u>The vibrations of thought.</u> Highly sexed people mix the emotion of sex with their thoughts, or may do so at will, and in that way, may influence those around them.
_____
_____

5. <u>Body adornment.</u> People who are highly sexed are usually very careful about their personal appearance. They usually select clothing of a style becoming to their personality, physique, complexion, etc.
_____
_____

TASK 5: GAIN CONTROL OF YOUR THOUGHTS

> The desire for sexual expression is by far the strongest and most impelling of all the human emotions, and for this very reason this desire, when harnessed and transmuted into action, other than that of physical expression, may raise one to the status of a genius.
>
> The road to genius consists of the development, control, and use of sex, love, and romance. Briefly, the process may be stated as follows: Encourage the presence of these emotions as the dominating thoughts in one's mind, and discourage the presence of all the destructive emotions. The mind is a creature of habit. It thrives upon the dominating thoughts fed it. Through the faculty of willpower, one may discourage the presence of any emotion, and encourage the presence of any other. Control of the mind, through the power of will, is not difficult. Control comes from persistence, and habit. The secret of control lies in understanding the process of transmutation. When any negative emotion presents itself in one's mind, it can be transmuted into a positive, or constructive emotion, by the simple procedure of changing one's thoughts.

List the negative thoughts and emotions you still have. Write them below and replace them with a positive thought. This is a practice of transmuting the old thoughts which do not serve you to new thoughts which do.

Old Negative Thought: _____
New Thought: _____

Old Negative Thought: _____
New Thought: _____

Old Negative Thought: _____
New Thought: _____

Old Negative Thought: _____
New Thought: _____

THERE IS NO OTHER ROAD TO GENIUS THAN THROUGH VOLUNTARY SELF-EFFORT!

11

The Eleventh Step Towards Riches

THE SUBCONSCIOUS MIND

The Connecting Link

> The subconscious mind consists of a field of consciousness in which every impulse of thought that reaches the objective mind through any of the five senses is classified and recorded, and from which thoughts may be recalled or withdrawn as letters may be taken from a filing cabinet.
>
> It receives and files sense impressions or thoughts, regardless of their nature. You may voluntarily plant in your subconscious mind any plan, thought, or purpose which you desire to translate into its physical or monetary equivalent. The subconscious acts first on the dominating desires which have been mixed with emotional feeling, such as faith.

THOUGHTS BACK OF IT

The subconscious mind consists of a field of consciousness, in which every impulse of thought that reaches the objective mind through any of the five senses, is classified and recorded, and from which thoughts may be recalled or withdrawn as letters may be taken from a filing cabinet.

It receives, and files, sense impressions or thoughts, regardless of their nature. You may voluntarily plant in your subconscious mind any plan, thought, or purpose which you desire to translate into its physical or monetary equivalent. The subconscious acts first on the dominating desires which have been mixed with emotional feeling, such as faith.

THE SEVEN MAJOR POSITIVE EMOTIONS

The emotion of **DESIRE**
The emotion of **FAITH**
The emotion of **LOVE**
The emotion of **SEX**
The emotion of **ENTHUSIASM**
The emotion of **ROMANCE**
The emotion of **HOPE**

THE SEVEN MAJOR NEGATIVE EMOTIONS

(to be avoided)

The emotion of **FEAR**
The emotion of **JEALOUSY**
The emotion of **HATRED**
The emotion of **REVENGE**
The emotion of **GREED**
The emotion of **SUPERSTITION**
The emotion of **ANGER**

THE BROADCASTING AND RECEIVING STATION

Every human brain is both a broadcasting and receiving station for the vibration of thought. Through the medium of the ether, in a fashion similar to that employed by the radio broadcasting principle, every human brain is capable of picking up vibrations of thought which are being released by other brains.

The Creative Imagination is the "receiving set" of the brain, which receives thoughts, released by the brains of others. It is the agency of communication between one's conscious, or reasoning mind, and the four sources from which one may receive thought stimuli.

When stimulated, or "stepped up" to a high rate of vibration, the mind becomes more receptive to the vibration of thought which reaches it through the ether from outside sources. This "stepping up" process takes place through the positive emotions, or the negative emotions. Through the emotions, the vibrations of thought may be increased.

Hill had discovered what he believed to be the ideal conditions under which the mind can be stimulated so that the sixth sense can be made to function in a practical way.

The conditions to which Hill refers consist of a close working alliance between himself and members of his staff. Through experimentation and practice, he had discovered how to stimulate their minds (by applying the principle used in connection with the "Invisible Counselors" described in the next chapter) so that they could, by a process of blending their three minds into one, find the solution to a great variety of personal problems which were submitted by his clients.

The procedure was very simple. They sat down at a conference table, clearly stated the nature of the problem they had under consideration, then began discussing it. Each contributed whatever thoughts that had occurred. The strange thing about this method of mind stimulation was that it placed each participant in communication with unknown sources of knowledge definitely outside of their own experience.

TASK 1: SEEDING POSITIVE EMOTIONS

Positive and negative emotions cannot occupy the mind at the same time. One or the other must dominate. It is your responsibility to make sure that positive emotions constitute the dominating influence of your mind. Here the law of HABIT will come to your aid. Form the habit of applying and using the positive emotions! Eventually, they will dominate your mind so completely that the negatives cannot enter it.

Consciously choose to complete the below sentences with positive statements and instill them with positive emotions. Repeat them daily, in your mind and aloud while moving your body. This practice will create new subconscious thought habits.

I am grateful for _____

_____

I believe _____

_____

I know _____

_____

I will _____

_____

I am open to receive _____

_____

THE 'MIXING' OF FAITH WITH A PLAN, OR PURPOSE, INTENDED FOR SUBMISSION TO THE SUBCONSCIOUS MIND, MAY BE DONE ONLY THROUGH THE IMAGINATION.

TASK 2: TRIGGERING SOLUTIONS FROM THE ETHER

Stating positive desires as a question inspires the mind to seek solutions from the four sources of stimuli.

Say the below statements with positive emotion daily, in your mind and aloud, while moving your body...

- Why is everything always working out for me?
- Why does money flow easily and abundantly to me?
- Why do my dreams organically become my reality?
- How does it get better than this?

List other WHY or HOW questions that align with your intended outcomes to create new thought habits.

_____

_____

_____

_____

_____

_____

_____

_____

_____

EVERYTHING WHICH MAN CREATES BEGINS IN THE FORM OF A THOUGHT IMPULSE.

TASK 3: CRAFTING YOUR DAILY THOUGHT RITUAL

> Through a method of procedure, unknown to man, the subconscious mind draws upon the forces of Infinite Intelligence for the power with which it voluntarily transmutes one's desire into their physical equivalent, making use always of the most practical media by which this end may be accomplished. You cannot entirely control your subconscious mind, but you can voluntarily hand over to it any plan, desire, or purpose which you wish transformed into concrete form.
>
> The subconscious mind is a medium for transmuting your desires into their physical or monetary equivalent. Remember the subconscious mind may be voluntarily directed only through HABIT, under the directions given in the chapter on faith. Be patient and persistent.

List the actions you will take daily repeatedly and in the spirit of faith instilled with emotion to create new thought habits which serves your life's purpose and vision.

Upon awaking each day, I will:

_____
_____
_____
_____
_____
_____

Upon laying to rest each night, I will:

_____
_____
_____
_____
_____
_____

MAN CAN CREATE NOTHING WHICH HE DOES NOT FIRST CONCEIVE IN THOUGHT.

"You never can tell what a thought will do in
bringing you hate or love - for thoughts are things,
and their airy wings are swifter than carrier doves.

They follow the law of the universe -
Each thing creates its kind,

And they speed o'er the track to bring you back
Whatever went out from your mind."

~ Ella Wheeler Wilcox ~

12

The Twelfth Step Towards Riches

THE BRAIN

A Broadcasting and Receiving Station for Thought

> The subconscious mind consists of a field of consciousness in which every impulse of thought that reaches the objective mind through any of the Under the right circumstances and in a fashion that may be likened to that employed by the radio broadcasting principle, every human brain is capable of "picking up" thought impulses which originate in the brains of others.

TASK 1: MASTERMIND EXERCISE

The Mastermind method of mind stimulation via a round-table procedure, through harmonious discussion of definite subjects, between three or more people, illustrates the simplest and most practical use of the Mastermind.

During your next Mastermind meeting, follow the steps applied by Napoleon Hill.

Begin by clearly stating the nature of any problem, challenge, or situation you are experiencing as it relates to your Statement of Desire, and then begin to discuss it as a group. This brainstorming session invites members to contribute whatever thoughts they may have; a mechanism of blending multiple minds into one for the purpose of finding solutions.

Take note of any significant thoughts as they are revealed;
explore them further.

_____
_____
_____
_____
_____
_____
_____
_____
_____
_____
_____
_____
_____
_____
_____

THOUGHT VIBRATIONS STEPPED UP WITH A MIND STIMULI ONE CAN ACCESS THE LEVEL OF GENIUS.

TASK 2: WEEKLY MASTERMIND PRACTICE

Continue your Mastermind practice following the steps applied by Napoleon Hill.

1. Clearly state the nature of any problem, challenge, or situation you are experiencing as it relates to your Statement of Desire.
2. Begin to discuss it as a group.
3. Take note of any significant thoughts as they are revealed.

_____
_____
_____
_____
_____
_____
_____
_____
_____
_____
_____
_____
_____
_____
_____
_____
_____
_____
_____
_____
_____
_____

ALL INDIVIDUALS HAVE BECOME WHAT THEY ARE BECAUSE OF THEIR DOMINATING THOUGHTS AND DESIRES.

13

The Thirteenth Step Towards Riches

THE SIXTH SENSE

The Door to the Temple of Wisdom

TASK 1: SELECT YOUR 'INVISIBLE COUNSELORS'

> List the names of each person you would like to emulate and the chief qualities you'd like to adopt from each of them. These 'Invisible Counselors' may be men or women, alive or dead, who inspire you, whom you admire, and whom you would like to learn from. Then form a mental picture of yourself sharing a round-table meeting with the group. Take note of any advice they may share with you in pursuit of attaining your Statement of Desire. Apply the principles of Faith, Imagination, and Persistence each time you host a meeting with your 'Invisible Counselors'.

Invisible Counselor #1: _____

Chief Qualities Include: _____
Advice I've Received: _____

Invisible Counselor #2: _____

Chief Qualities Include: _____
Advice I've Received: _____

Invisible Counselor #3: _____

Chief Qualities Include: _____
Advice I've Received: _____

Invisible Counselor #4: _____

Chief Qualities Include: _____
Advice I've Received: _____

Invisible Counselor #5: _____

Chief Qualities Include: _____
Advice I've Received: _____

Invisible Counselor #6: _____

Chief Qualities Include: _____
Advice I've Received: _____

THE APEX OF THE THINK AND GROW RICH PHILOSOPHY

The "thirteenth" principle is known as the SIXTH SENSE, through which Infinite Intelligence may, and will communicate voluntarily, without any effort from, or demands by, the individual.

This principle is the apex of the philosophy. It can be assimilated, understood, and applied ONLY by first mastering the other twelve principles.

The Sixth Sense is that portion of the subconscious mind which has been referred to as the Creative Imagination. It has also been referred to as the "receiving set" through which ideas, plans, and thoughts flash into the mind. The "flashes" are sometimes called "hunches" or "inspirations."

Understanding of the sixth sense comes only by meditation through mind development from within. The sixth sense probably is the medium of contact between the finite mind of man and Infinite Intelligence, and for this reason, it is a mixture of both the mental and the spiritual. It is believed to be the point at which the mind of man contacts the Universal Mind.

TASK 2: BUILDING CHARACTER THROUGH AUTOSUGGESTION

Who we are is an effect of who we are being - how we are behaving; our thoughts, actions, and emotional vibration. Examples include: "I am a giver", "I feel enthusiastic", "I believe in myself and others", "I have a positive and helpful attitude".

Consciously choose the person you desire to become!

I am _____

I am _____

I am _____

I feel _____

I feel _____

I feel _____

I believe _____

I believe _____

I believe _____

I have _____

I have _____

I have _____

My ways of being are...

_____

_____

_____

_____

_____

INVISIBLE COUNSELORS

"My experience has taught me that the next best thing to being truly great is to emulate the great by feeling and action, as nearly as possible. Long before I had ever written a line for publication, or endeavored to deliver a speech in public, I followed the habit of reshaping my own character, by trying to imitate the nine men whose lives and life-works had been most impressive to me. These nine men were, Emerson, Paine, Edison, Darwin, Lincoln, Burbank, Napoleon, Ford, and Carnegie. Every night, over a long period of years, I held an imaginary Council meeting with this group whom I called my "Invisible Counselors."

The procedure was this: Just before going to sleep at night, I would shut my eyes, and see, in my imagination, this group of men seated with me around my Council Table. Here I had not only an opportunity to sit among those whom I considered to be great, but I actually dominated the group, by serving as the Chairman.

I had a very DEFINITE PURPOSE in indulging my imagination through these nightly meetings. My purpose was to rebuild my own character so it would represent a composite of the characters of my imaginary counselors. Realizing, as I did, early in life, that I had to overcome the handicap of birth in an environment of ignorance and superstition, I deliberately assigned myself the task of voluntary rebirth through the method here described.

Being an earnest student of psychology, I knew, of course, that all men have become what they are, because of their DOMINATING THOUGHTS AND DESIRES. I knew that every deeply seated desire has the effect of causing one to seek outward expression through which that desire may be transmuted into reality. I knew that self-suggestion is a powerful factor in building character, that it is, in fact, the sole principle through which character is built. With this knowledge of the principles of mind operation, I was fairly well armed with the equipment needed in rebuilding my character. In these imaginary Council meetings, I called on my Cabinet members for the knowledge I wished each to contribute, addressing myself to each member in audible words. My method of addressing the members of the imaginary Cabinet would vary, according to the traits of character in which I was, for the moment, most interested in acquiring. After some months of this nightly procedure, I was astounded by the discovery that these imaginary figures became, apparently real."

Epilogue

Take Inventory of Yourself

HOW TO OUTWIT THE 6 GHOSTS OF FEAR

Laying Challenges to Rest

THE MASTERY OF FEAR

Take inventory of yourself as you read this closing chapter and find out how many of the "Ghosts" are standing in your way. Before you can put any portion of this philosophy into successful use, your mind must be prepared to receive it. The preparation is not difficult. It begins with study, analysis, and understanding of three enemies which you shall have to clear out.

These are **indecision, doubt,** and **fear!**

Fears are nothing more than states of mind. One's state of mind is subject to control and direction. Nature has endowed man with absolute control over but one thing, and that is THOUGHT. This fact, coupled with the additional fact that everything which man creates, begins in the form of a thought, leads one very near to the principle by which FEAR may be mastered.

- The fear of **POVERTY**

- The fear of **CRITICISM**

- The fear of **ILL HEALTH**

- The fear of **LOSS OF LOVE OF SOMEONE**

- The fear of **OLD AGE**

- The fear of **DEATH**

You may control your own mind; you have the power to feed it whatever thought impulses you choose. With this privilege also comes the responsibility of using it constructively. You are the master of your own earthly destiny just as surely as you have the power to control your own thoughts.

INDECISION IS THE SEEDLING OF FEAR! INDECISION CRYSTALLIZES DOUBT. THE TWO BLENDED TOGETHER, BECOME FEAR.

TASK 1: ACKNOWLEDGE YOUR FEARS

> Fears are the slayer of dreams. Before we can master an enemy, we must know its name, its habits, and its place of abode. As you read, analyze yourself carefully and determine which, if any, of these six common fears have attached themselves to you.

List the thoughts and beliefs that you have around each of the below six fears. Write how each of these fears has held you back or stopped you from taking action towards attainment of your dreams. What is the impact each has had on your life?

The fear of **POVERTY**

Belief: _____
Impact: _____

The fear of **CRITICISM**

Belief: _____
Impact: _____

The fear of **ILL HEALTH**

Belief: _____
Impact: _____

The fear of **LOSS OF LOVE OF SOMEONE**

Belief: _____
Impact: _____

The fear of **OLD AGE**

Belief: _____
Impact: _____

The fear of **DEATH**

Belief: _____
Impact: _____

TASK 2: PROTECT YOURSELF AGAINST NEGATIVE INFLUENCES

Daily Practice

Protect yourself against negative influences, whether of your own making, or the result of the activities of negative people around you, recognize that you have a willpower, and put it into constant use, until it builds a wall of immunity against negative influences in your own mind.

Recognize the fact that you, and every other human being, are, by nature, lazy, indifferent, and susceptible to all suggestions which harmonize with your weaknesses.

Recognize that you are, by nature, susceptible to all the six basic fears, and set up habits for the purpose of counteracting all these fears.

Recognize that negative influences often work on you through your subconscious mind, therefore, they are difficult to detect, and keep your mind closed against all people who depress or discourage you in any way.

Clean out your medicine chest, throw away all pill bottles, and stop pandering to colds, aches, pains and imaginary illness.

Deliberately seek the company of people who influence you to think and act for yourself.

Do not expect troubles as they have a tendency not to disappoint.

Without doubt, the most common weakness of all human beings is the habit of leaving their minds open to the negative influence of other people. This weakness is all the more damaging, because most people do not recognize that they are cursed by it, and many who acknowledge it, neglect or refuse to correct the evil until it becomes an uncontrollable part of their daily habits.

THE MOST COMMON WEAKNESS OF ALL HUMAN BEINGS IS THE HABIT OF LEAVING THEIR MINDS OPEN TO THE NEGATIVE INFLUENCE OF OTHER PEOPLE.

SELF-ANALYSIS TEST QUESTIONS

> To aid those who wish to see themselves as they really are, the following list of questions has been prepared. Read the questions and state your answers aloud so you can hear your own voice. This will make it easier for you to be truthful with yourself. If you have answered all these questions truthfully, you know more about yourself than the majority of people. Study the questions carefully, come back to them once each week for several months, and be astounded at the amount of additional knowledge of great value to yourself, you will have gained by the simple method of answering the questions truthfully. If you are not certain concerning the answers to some of the questions, seek the counsel of those who know you well, especially those who have no motive in flattering you, and see yourself through their eyes. The experience will be astonishing.

1. Do you complain often of "feeling bad," and if so, what is the cause?

2. Do you find fault with other people at the slightest provocation?

3. Do you frequently make mistakes in your work, and if so, why?

4. Are you sarcastic and offensive in your conversation?

5. Do you deliberately avoid the association of anyone, and if so, why?

6. Do you suffer frequently with indigestion? If so, what is the cause?

7. Does life seem futile and the future hopeless to you? If so, why?

8. Do you like your occupation? If not, why?

9. Do you often feel self-pity, and if so why?

10. Are you envious of those who excel you?

11. To which do you devote most time, thinking of success, or of failure?

12. Are you gaining or losing self-confidence as you grow older?

13. Do you learn something of value from all mistakes?

14. Are you permitting some relative or acquaintance to worry you? If so, why?

15. Are you sometimes "in the clouds" and at other times in the depths of despondency?

16. Who has the most inspiring influence upon you? What is the cause?

17. Do you tolerate negative or discouraging influences which you can avoid?

18. Are you careless of your personal appearance? If so, when and why?

19. Have you learned how to "drown your troubles" by being too busy to be annoyed by them?

20. Would you call yourself a "spineless weakling" if you permitted others to do your thinking for you?

21. Do you neglect internal bathing until auto-intoxication makes you ill-tempered and irritable?

22. How many preventable disturbances annoy you, and why do you tolerate them?

23. Do you resort to liquor, narcotics, or cigarettes to "quiet your nerves"? If so, why do you not try willpower instead?

24. Does anyone "nag" you, and if so, for what reason?

25. Do you have a Definite Chief Aim in Life, and if so, what is it, and what plan have you for achieving it?

26. Do you suffer from any of the Six Basic Fears? If so, which ones?

27. Have you a method by which you can shield yourself against the negative influence of others?

28. Do you make deliberate use of autosuggestion to make your mind positive?

29. Which do you value most, your material possessions, or your privilege of controlling your own thoughts?

30. Are you easily influenced by others, against your own judgment?

31. Has today added anything of value to your stock of knowledge or state of mind?

32. Do you face squarely the circumstances which make you unhappy, or sidestep the responsibility?

33. Do you analyze all mistakes and failures and try to profit by them or, do you take the attitude that this is not your duty?

34. Can you name three of your most damaging weaknesses? What are you doing to correct them?

35. Do you encourage other people to bring their worries to you for sympathy?

36. Do you choose, from your daily experiences, lessons or influences which aid in your personal advancement?

37. Does your presence have a negative influence on other people as a rule?

38. What habits of other people annoy you most?

39. Do you form your own opinions or permit yourself to be influenced by other people?

40. Have you learned how to create a mental state of mind with which you can shield yourself against all discouraging influences?

41. Does your occupation inspire you with faith and hope?

42. Are you conscious of possessing spiritual forces of sufficient power to enable you to keep your mind free from all forms of fear?

43. Does your religion help you to keep your own mind positive?

44. Do you feel it your duty to share other people's worries? If so, why?

45. If you believe that "birds of a feather flock together" what have you learned about yourself by studying the friends whom you attract?

46. What connection, if any, do you see between the people with whom you associate most closely, and any unhappiness you may experience?

47. Could it be possible that some person whom you consider to be a friend is, in reality, your worst enemy, because of his negative influence on your mind?

48. By what rules do you judge who is helpful and who is damaging to you?

49. Are your intimate associates mentally superior or inferior to you?

50. How much time out of every 24 hours do you devote to:

   a. your occupation

   b. sleep

   c. play and relaxation

   d. acquiring useful knowledge

   e. plain waste

51. Who among your acquaintances,

   a. encourages you most

   b. cautions you most

   c. discourages you most

   d. helps you most in other ways

52. What is your greatest worry? Why do you tolerate it?

53. When others offer you free, unsolicited advice, do you accept it without question, or analyze their motive?

54. What, above all else, do you most desire?

55. Do you intend to acquire it?

56. Are you willing to subordinate all other desires for this one?

57. How much time daily do you devote to acquiring it?

58. Do you change your mind often? If so, why?

59. Do you usually finish everything you begin?

60. Are you easily impressed by other people's business or professional titles, college, degrees, or wealth?

61. Are you easily influenced by what other people think or say of you?

62. Do you cater to people because of their social or financial status?

63. Whom do you believe is the greatest person living?

64. In what respect is this person superior to yourself?

65. How much time have you devoted to studying and answering these questions?

WHAT QUESTIONS HAVE YOU NOT YET ASKED YOURSELF THAT WOULD SERVE YOU

Write a list of additional questions below. Use your imagination.

1.

2.

3.

4.

5.

6.

7.

8.

9.

10.

57 FAMOUS ALIBIS

BY OLD MAN 'IF'

> People who do not succeed have one distinguishing trait in common. They know all the reasons for failure, and have what they believe to be airtight alibis to explain away their own lack of achievement. Some of these alibis are clever, and a few of them are justifiable by the facts but alibis cannot be used for money. The world wants to know only one thing, have you achieved success? A character analyst compiled a list of the most commonly used alibis. As you read the list, examine yourself carefully, and determine how many of these alibis, if any, are your own property. Remember, too, the philosophy presented in this book makes every one of these alibis obsolete.

IF I didn't have a wife and family . . .

IF I had enough "pull" . . .

IF I had money . . .

IF I had a good education . . .

IF I could get a job . . .

IF I had good health . . .

IF I only had time . . .

IF times were better . . .

IF other people understood me . . .

IF conditions around me were only different . . .

IF I could live my life over again . . .

IF I did not fear what "THEY" would say . . .

IF I had been given a chance . . .

IF I now had a chance . . .

IF other people didn't "have it in for me" . . .

IF nothing happens to stop me . . .

IF I were only younger . . .

IF I could only do what I want . . .

IF I had been born rich . . .

IF I could meet "the right people" . . .

IF I had the talent that some people have . . .

IF I dared assert myself . . .

IF I only had embraced past opportunities . . .

IF people didn't get on my nerves . . .

IF I didn't have to keep house and look after the children . . .

IF I could save some money . . .

IF the boss only appreciated me . . .

IF I only had somebody to help me . . .

IF my family understood me . . .

IF I lived in a big city . . .

IF I could just get started . . .

IF I were only free . . .

IF I had the personality of some people . . .

IF I were not so fat . . .

IF my talents were known . . .

IF I could just get a "break" . . .

IF I could only get out of debt . . .

IF I hadn't failed . . .

IF I only knew how . . .

IF everybody didn't oppose me . . .

IF I didn't have so many worries . . .

IF I could marry the right person . . .

IF people weren't so dumb . . .

IF my family were not so extravagant . . .

IF I were sure of myself . . .

IF luck were not against me . . .

IF I had not been born under the wrong star . . .

IF it were not true that "what is to be will be" . . .

IF I did not have to work so hard . . .

IF I hadn't lost my money . . .

IF I lived in a different neighborhood . . .

IF I didn't have a "past" . . .

IF I only had a business of my own . . .

IF other people would only listen to me . . .

IF (and this is the greatest of them all) I had the courage to see myself as I really am, I would find out what is wrong with me and correct it, then I might have a chance to profit by my mistakes and to learn something from the experience of others; for I know that there is something wrong with me, or I would now be where I would have been IF I had spent more time analyzing my weaknesses and less time building alibis to cover them.

Building alibis with which to explain away failure is a national pastime. The habit is as old as the human race and is fatal to success! Why do people cling to their pet alibis? The answer is obvious. They defend their alibis because they create them! A person's alibis are the children of their own imagination. It is human nature to defend one's own brainchild.

Building alibis is a deeply rooted habit. Habits are difficult to break, especially when they provide justification for something we do. Plato had this truth in mind when he said, "The first and best victory is to conquer self. To be conquered by self is, of all things, the most shameful and vile."

Another philosopher had the same thought in mind when he said, "It was a great surprise to me when I discovered that most of the ugliness I saw in others was but a reflection of my own nature."

SUCCESS NOTES

SUCCESS NOTES

SUCCESS NOTES

SUCCESS NOTES

SUCCESS NOTES

SUCCESS NOTES

ABOUT THE AUTHOR

Janine M. Loweth

... is a dynamic soul who operates from love, kindness and team. She is a sales executive and artist-turned-author, passionate about human connection and committed to creating a world where every person gets that they matter.

She is a dedicated mother, a loving family member (to those both chosen & genetic), a loyal friend and helping hand to all. Janine Loweth was born in Flatbush, New York, to what she had believed was an Italian American family (equipped with heavy Brooklyn accents - Ay! Oh!) until a DNA test had declared she was, in fact, a citizen of the world (essentially a walking-talking version of ancestry soup). She was raised in and continues to reside in New Jersey (accent free-ish).

A graduate of the Fashion Institute of Technology and Montclair State University, her 25+ year career has been a spectrum of color. A self-declared Connection Advocate, Janine has helped new and expectant parents (in preparation of their next chapter), homeowners (to create the environment of their dreams), small and mid-sized business owners and their clientele (to reach and surpass their goals), enterprise businesses (to create ease and efficiencies), locally, nationally and internationally (across a broad variety of industries) and she has done so reliably, honestly, and responsibly.

Janine has led cross-state projects such as: Appalachian Illumination and local initiatives such as Free the Birds. She is the President of J9 Consulting LLC, has held leadership roles in her local lake community, a Steering Committee leader at The Paterson Film & Entertainment Commission, and author of the *Roadmap to Success* Workbook inspired by her experience of Napoleon Hill's masterpiece Think and Grow Rich, which had helped her to gain clarity of her purpose. Janine has since released the Human Doctrine, *I AM,* to the world. It's simple yet powerful message shares that humanity is and can be united by access to fundamental ways of being that can be experienced and practiced by people of all ages.

www.IAmChildrenBooks.com

REFERENCES

- Think and Grow Rich by Napoleon Hill
- The One Thing by Gary Keller
- The Power of the Subconscious Mind by Dr. Joseph Murphy
- Your Infinite Power to Be Rich by Dr. Joseph Murphy
- Content from Tony Robbins
- Access Consciousness by Gary Douglas
- BOLD by Maps Coaching
- Content from Carolyn Elliott